Praise for
Parent Voice

Parents often struggle to find the right way to use their own voice in supporting, nurturing, and advocating for their children at home and at school. This book provides important wisdom from experienced educators that incorporates deep knowledge of children's needs and development to help parents listen to their children, learn from them, and lead them toward becoming self-reliant adults.

—Gerald Aungst, K–4 Gifted Teacher
Cheltenham Elementary School
Cheltenham, PA

Parent Voice *opens up a good dialogue between parents and educators that can facilitate better communication.*

—Leslie Standerfer, High School Principal
Estrella Foothills High School
Goodyear, AZ

Parent Voice *describes how to handle difficult situations with the "Listen, Learn, Lead" structure, and also offers solutions to prevent them in the first place. This book teaches parents how to use their voices in effective ways and how to give their children voice.*

—Karen L. Tichy, EdD, Assistant Professor
of Educational Leadership
Saint Louis University
St. Louis, MO

Parent Voice

*Whether they realize it or not, our children gave us
the inspiration and courage to write this book.
Lauren, Casey, Chelsea, Cali, Adlee, Andrew, and Brayden
—always know that you not only have our hearts but also our ears.
We listen to and learn from your voices every day!
(And no, this does not mean you'll be receiving
a percentage of the royalties!)*

Parent Voice

Being in Tune With Your Kids and Their School

Russell J. Quaglia

Kristine Fox

Deborah Young

A SAGE Publishing Company

A SAGE Publishing Company

FOR INFORMATION:

Corwin
A SAGE Company
2455 Teller Road
Thousand Oaks, California 91320
(800) 233-9936
www.corwin.com

SAGE Publications Ltd.
1 Oliver's Yard
55 City Road
London EC1Y 1SP
United Kingdom

SAGE Publications India Pvt. Ltd.
B 1/I 1 Mohan Cooperative Industrial Area
Mathura Road, New Delhi 110 044
India

SAGE Publications Asia-Pacific Pte. Ltd.
3 Church Street
#10-04 Samsung Hub
Singapore 049483

Publisher: Arnis Burvikovs
Senior Developmental Editor: Desirée
                                A. Bartlett
Editorial Assistant: Kaitlyn Irwin
Production Editor: Amy Schroller
Copy Editor: Jocelyn Rau
Typesetter: C&M Digitals (P) Ltd.
Proofreader: Laura Webb
Indexer: Maria Sosnowski
Cover Designer: Candice Harman
Marketing Manager: Nicole Franks

Printed in the United States of America

ISBN: 978-1-5063-6010-2

This book is printed on acid-free paper.

Certified Chain of Custody
SUSTAINABLE   Promoting Sustainable Forestry
FORESTRY
INITIATIVE   www.sfiprogram.org
               SFI-01268
SFI label applies to text stock

17 18 19 20 21 10 9 8 7 6 5 4 3 2 1

Contents

ACKNOWLEDGMENTS   xi

ABOUT THE AUTHORS   xiii

NOTE FROM DR. Q   xvii

INTRODUCTION: BE THE PARENT YOU
WANT TO BE . . . AND THE PARENT
YOUR CHILDREN DESERVE!   1

    1. NOISE OR VOICE?   7

       The New Language   10

       The Responsibility of Voice   12

       Mom's Musings on Voice   14

       Dad's Deliberations on Voice   16

       Tuning Into Your Own Voice   18

       Now Hear This!   19

    2. LISTEN: HEARING THE RIGHT NOTES   21

       Listening Matters   24

       Keys to Effective Listening   26

       Mom's Musings on Listening   33

       Dad's Deliberations on Listening   35

       Listening: Take Action   37

Listening Through the Years   42

In Their Own Words: Advice on Listening,
    From Children to Parents   46

Listening for Life   49

3. LEARN: GETTING IN RHYTHM   51

Learning Matters   54

Mindful Learning   55

Learning and Interests   56

Speaking Their Language   57

Shared Adventures   59

Keys to Sincere Learning   61

Mom's Musings on Learning   66

Dad's Deliberations on Learning   68

Learning: Take Action   70

Learning Through the Years   74

Our Learning From Parents and Children   78

Never Stop Learning   80

4. LEAD: WORKING IN HARMONY WITH YOUR CHILD AND SCHOOL   83

Leading Matters   85

Digging Deeper   87

Developing Partnerships   88

Shared Goals   91

Keys to Leading Successfully   93

Proactive Voice at School   97

Mom's Musings on Leading   100

Dad's Deliberations on Leading   102

Leading: Take Action   104

Leading Through the Years   108

Our Learning About Leading   112

We Are All in This Together   115

5. STAYING IN TUNE WITH YOUR
   CHILD AND SCHOOL   117

Accept and Respect the Fact That Your Children
     Have Different Perspectives Than You   118

Parents Need and Deserve a Meaningful Role in School   118

Parenting Should Be a Priority, All the Time   119

Be Intentional   119

Be Yourself   120

INDEX   121

Acknowledgments

Corwin gratefully acknowledges the contributions of the following reviewers:

Gerald Aungst, K-4 Gifted Teacher
Cheltenham Elementary School
Cheltenham, PA

Marsha L. Carr, Associate Professor/Ed Leadership and
    Doctorate Coordinator for EdAdmin
University of North Carolina Wilmington
Wilmington, NC

Leslie Standerfer, High School Principal
Estrella Foothills High School
Goodyear, AZ

Karen L. Tichy, EdD, Assistant Professor of Educational
    Leadership
Saint Louis University
St. Louis, MO

About the Authors

 **Russell J. Quaglia** is a globally recognized pioneer in the field of education, known for his unwavering dedication to Student Voice and Aspirations. Dr. Quaglia has been described by news media as "America's foremost authority on the development and achievement of student voice and aspirations." His innovative work is evidenced by an extensive library of researched-based publications, prominent international speaking appearances, and a successfully growing list of aspirations ventures.

Among these ventures, Dr. Quaglia authored the School Voice suite of surveys, including *Student Voice, Teacher Voice, Parent Voice* and *iKnow My Class.* His books, *Engagement by Design; Aspire High: Imagining Tomorrow's School Today; Student Voice: The Instrument of Change; Principal Voice: Listen, Learn, Lead;* and *Teacher Voice: Amplifying Success* have received international acclaim.

In addition to founding and leading the Quaglia Institute for Student Aspirations, Dr. Quaglia also founded the Aspirations Academies Trust, a sponsor of primary and secondary academies in England built on his aspirations research. Most recently, he has founded the Teacher Voice and Aspirations International Center, dedicated to amplifying the voice of teachers for them to realize their aspirations and reach their fullest potential.

Dr. Quaglia earned his bachelor's degree at Assumption College, a master's degree in economics from Boston College, and master of education and doctorate degrees from Columbia University, specializing in the area of organizational theory and behavior. He has been awarded numerous honorary doctorates in humanitarian services for his dedication to students. Dr. Quaglia's work has also led him to serve on several national and international committees, reflecting his passion for ensuring that Student, Teacher, and Parent Voice are always heard, honored, and acted upon.

Kristine Fox is a Senior Field Specialist/Research Associate for the Quaglia Institute for Student Aspirations. Dr. Fox received her doctorate from The University of Maine in Educational Leadership, EdM from Harvard University and BA from The University of Michigan. She co-authored with Dr. Quaglia *8 Conditions That Make a Difference* and *Aspire High: Imagining Tomorrow's School Today* (Corwin, 2017), and has published in *Educational Leadership, American School Board Journal, ASCD Express* and *Principal Magazine*. For more than a decade she has worked diligently with students, teachers, and administrators to incorporate student voice as a fundamental necessity in school improvement efforts. Dr. Fox previously was a K-8 administrator and 6-12 teacher.

Deborah Young is the Director of Operations and Program Specialist for the Quaglia Institute for Student Aspirations (QISA). Deborah earned her Master of Education degree from Smith College. She has teaching experience in both public and private schools. Early in her career, Deborah's experience in the classroom strengthened the belief that initially drew her to the teaching profession: every child deserves the opportunity to achieve his or her aspirations, and teachers can make a tremendous difference in helping students do just that. Her decisions as a teacher were based on a core belief that mutual respect between teachers and students is essential to creating a positive learning environment. A key aspect of such respect is the ability, and responsibility, of educators to honor and respond to student voice. Deborah's work at QISA proves to be a continuation of her commitment to honoring student voice as a vital component of creating school environments that foster students' aspirations.

Note from Dr. Q

There are literally hundreds, if not thousands, of books on parenting. A simple Google search will highlight "how to" guides for everything from making homemade baby food to sewing Halloween costumes with your kids to helping your high school senior write college essays. The last thing I ever thought I would do is write a book on parenting. My first book, *Believing in Achieving*, written over 20 years ago with Dr. Fox, was about student aspirations and the conditions in schools that affect student development. It set the stage for books that followed, including *Student Voice: The Instrument of Change; Teacher Voice: Amplifying Success; Aspire High: Imagining Tomorrow's School Today*; and *Principal Voice: Listen, Learn, Lead*. I believed the only thing necessary to bring about significant change in school was the voices of students, teachers, and principals. Throughout the journey, however, I received constant inquiries about parent voice. Not just from parents but my colleagues at the Institute: "What about the voices of parents?" "You can't ignore the impact of parents." "Parents need a voice, too!"

So what took me so long? First, I never put myself in the "parenting expert" category. Second, as a former school administrator, I thought parents had *too much* voice already. Third (and this is a confession of sorts…), my expertise was on student voice, and while parent voice obviously has an impact on students, I considered it tangential—not necessary and not missed by anyone. My second confession: I clearly remember telling parents during my days as a teacher and principal: "I want to hear from you," "What you think matters," and my favorite, "Please come in anytime so we can talk." The truth is, the last thing I wanted was an overinvolved parent in my room telling me how to teach or lead a school.

Alas, a few decades have passed, leading to my final confession: I was wrong on two accounts. Parent voice is far from tangential, and there is not too much of it. Parents deserve a voice, no matter how much has already been heard by any administrator. Parent voice has a profound impact on their children—in and outside of school.

To be clear, this book does *not* fit into the "how to" category of parenting. It is not, by any means, an instructional guide on being the perfect parent. It is a book designed to spur conversations between parents, educators, and, most importantly, your children in grades Prekindergarten through Grade 12. The three authors approached this book from various perspectives . . . parents, stepparents, and even grandparents. We have raised boys and girls whose ages range from 32 years old to a newborn (the grandchild!).

From the onset, I want you to understand that we are not approaching this book as parenting gurus. Being a parent is a learning adventure filled with many successes and even more challenges. Writing this book forced us to look back on the instances when we wished we had reacted differently, provided more support, or simply taken a deep breath before doing or saying anything. In the process of writing, we found ourselves not only reflecting on those moments but reflecting *in the moment* about how we could handle a situation differently. We hope this book does the same for other parents—that it starts you thinking and reflecting on your parenting abilities and how your voice, and the voice of your children, can play a role in successful parenting and developing and maintaining a positive relationship with school. While this book is primarily written for parents, we believe that educators can glean insights into how to better support parents and build strong home-school relationships.

I speak for both Kris and Deb (two of the best parents on the planet) when I say that we wholeheartedly believe there is no single correct way to parent. While we hope for similar outcomes for our children—*that they grow up to be happy, compassionate, fulfilled individuals who contribute positively to their communities*—we have different parenting styles. And each of our children have different personalities, abilities, hopes, and dreams. As we strive to do our best to support them in their own growth, we continually learn from them. For that, we are forever grateful.

Throughout this book, we use the term "parent" in the broadest sense. To us, parents include all caregivers who love and support children—stepparents, grandparents, guardians, foster parents, older siblings, family friends, and individuals in countless other roles who provide parental support. "Parenting" is an all-inclusive term for anyone who is in the role of loving and raising a child. In our professional lives, we have been fortunate to interview thousands of students, teachers, and parents. Those interviews and our experiences in schools have informed our ideas and insights related to parent voice.

As educators, the three of us have worked in schools for a combined total of almost a century. During that time, in our various roles—as teachers, administrators, community advocates, school volunteers, and school board members—we have partnered with countless parents in one way or another. We know that successful partnerships do not magically occur. Parents, children, and educators must work collaboratively to consciously develop trusting and meaningful relationships for the benefit of the students. Our school-based efforts and research at the Quaglia Institute focus on developing Voice: Voice for students, teachers, principals, and now parents. We believe that voice is a powerful resource. When used productively, voice leads to trust and respect within relationships, a sense of responsibility, authentic learning, and ultimately the confidence to pursue one's hopes and dreams. In previous work, I developed a School Voice Model that involves a process known as Listen, Learn, and Lead. This book introduces readers to the importance of each component and includes ideas for fostering parent-child-school relationships throughout the process.

We realize that just as caregiving roles and styles can vary, parenting is a unique experience with each child. No matter how close in age or circumstances children are, each child, and the parent's relationship with that child, is different. Regardless of the variances and variables—whether a child is an extrovert who befriends everyone or an introvert who prefers to keep a low profile, a prolific reader or a struggling math student, a student who loves formal schooling or a student who prefers alternative education—she deserves to have her voice heard. We hope *Parent Voice: Being in Tune With Your Kids and Their School* provides the support and inspiration parents need to ensure their voice and their children's voices are heard, respected, and valued. I apologize it took me so long to write about it!

Dr. Russell J. Quaglia

Introduction

Be the Parent *You* Want to Be . . . and the Parent *Your* Children Deserve!

"I will never do that!" Think back to the days before you were a parent—a time when you observed a mom in line at the grocery store finally giving in and buying her child that longed-for candy bar, or the occasion when you suffered through someone else's screaming toddler during dinner at a nice restaurant. Do you remember thinking to yourself, "I will *never* do *that* when I am a parent!"? Still feel the same way? All the best intentions, all the "I will never..." or "I will always...." promises made to oneself before actually becoming a parent are hard to keep. Those were the hypothetical moments. But parenthood is anything but hypothetical. We cannot anticipate every occurrence, or exactly how we'll respond to each event, while raising our children. Every day, hour, or minute is filled with ups and downs. Moments that are the most rewarding or the most frustrating. As one close friend put it just months after his first children were born (twins!), "It is absolutely the best thing I have ever done in my life. It is also the most challenging thing I have ever done." How true.

We, ourselves, have found navigating the path of parenthood to be an ongoing learning process—sometimes we are prepared for the moment right in front of us, other times we find ourselves scrambling in real time to find the right way to guide and support our children, both at home and at school. Throughout it all, we have learned that there is no *one* correct way to teach a child to read, reassure an insecure child, support a child whose parent is deployed, or help a child who experiences the loss of a loved one. There is no precise age that is best for experiencing that first sleepover, the first walk to the store without an adult, or the first date. Each of us has placed phone calls to friends and school counselors seeking advice on the right age for those milestone firsts.

We interact with and learn from parents and children in many different ways, both in our personal and professional lives. Every interaction and piece of advice has helped us grow as parents and educators. Before we had children, the roles varied—teacher, principal, babysitter, camp counselor, tutor, coach, aunt, uncle, and day care teacher. Once we became parents, our roles expanded to include self-taught counselors, internet-certified doctors, expert cleaners of every possible stain on every possible item, nutritionists, and unpaid taxi drivers. We experienced and learned from other parents about the challenges of talking with children about divorce, death, Internet dangers, protests, and current events that are a real part of our children's lives. Parenting is anything but simple or scripted.

We have learned that parenting is not predictable, and it is a different experience for every parent—even those parenting the same child. We have learned that so much in parenting involves multiple variables—dependent on the child's personality and level of responsibility, the parent's disposition, the comfort level of parent and child, and the other individuals involved. Some decisions are clear-cut with obvious answers: "No, you cannot go see the R-rated movie with your brother. He is 17 and you're 7!" Others are a bit murkier: "Your curfew is 10 o'clock because that seems like a reasonable time." "You want to go where and with whom to do what?" The latter category takes more thought—consideration of all those variables and reliance on your own experiences and what you have learned from talking with other parents. And, of course, we cannot disregard the "gut feeling" resource—the one that can be right even when we can't explain exactly why.

There are always variables to consider, and there is no single correct way to parent. There are as many perspectives as there are parents and as many personalities as there are children. The path is different for each parent and child, and it is a continual learning process. There is a general framework, however, that can assist with individualizing the process. The three fundamental components of the Voice Model (Quaglia, 2016) serve to foster mutual trust and respect, and a sense of responsibility: *Listen, Learn,* and *Lead.*

The Voice Model Represents a Process That Allows You to Develop Your and Your Child's Voice in a Manner That Builds Trust and Respect.

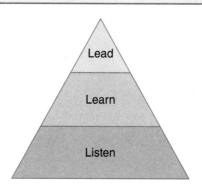

Listen: The foundation for supporting voice is all about listening. Chapter 2 highlights the notion that listening involves more than hearing someone else. It requires being fully engaged in the conversation. Listening is an active process that demonstrates you value the ideas and opinions of others.

Learn: Effective listening leads to meaningful learning. Chapter 3 shows that learning from our children shows them that we are interested in and respect *their* ideas and *their* interests. This simultaneously fosters mutual trust and respect. Underlying all of this is the fundamental belief that parents can learn a great deal from their children.

Lead: With a strong foundation of listening and learning, parents and children are better prepared to lead together. It is important for parents to model effective decision making, as well as provide opportunities for children to be responsible and make their own decisions. Chapter 4 explains the intricate details of leading with your children and engaging in parent-student-school partnerships.

For this approach to make a difference for you and your children, you need to be ready to believe that:

- Every child is wonderfully unique;
- Every child has something to teach us;
- Every child has the right to be respected, valued, and treated with dignity;
- Every child has his or her own dreams and aspirations;
- All parents care about their children;
- There is no single correct way to be a parent, and no parent is infallible;

- Parents want their voices to be heard by their children and at school;
- Partnerships and collaboration are better than detachment and isolation; and
- Schools want parents to be involved but do not always know how to engage all parents.

Belief in all of these—or the willingness to try to understand and believe them—is fundamental to the effectiveness of the Listen, Learn, Lead approach.

Parents have the power to make a difference; in fact, by virtue of their role, they *have the responsibility* to make a difference in their children's lives. Parents may not be featured in the latest viral video or seen hoisting the championship trophy to the crowd in celebration, and they may not be the face of the new brand of high-fashion sneakers, but that is fine. Parents are much more than that. Rather than being hero figures to be admired from afar, they are the everyday influences in their children's lives. They are the accessible, tangible heroes who can make a difference every day, and it can start by honoring voice (your child's and your own).

CHAPTER 1

Noise or Voice?

At one time or another, all parents experience the feeling of being invisible to their children. There are occasions when it feels like our children can hear everyone and everything *except* us. They hear the ice cream truck jingle from miles away, respond to the ring of their cell phones no matter the surrounding noise level, and attentively listen to the latest Instagram or YouTube star. Yet, they are quite adept at tuning out parents' voices. No matter how clearly we speak, our words are often background noise to our children. The question is, how can we help them tune in?

The concept of voice is not foreign to our children. Countless voices in different mediums compete for their "airtime," and those voices are often at their fingertips. Today's youth experience voice in ways unimaginable to earlier generations (particularly for those who believed children were better seen than heard!). Their voices can be expressed, discussed, and commented on at any time, all the time. They have 24/7 access to online forums, including blogs, videos, and petitions. Not only are children heard, but they are ready and willing to take action. Elementary students start GoFundMe or Kickstarter campaigns to raise money for important causes. Middle school students make a difference through online petitions at Change.org. High school students tweet their voices to share common concerns, stage protests, or share their peers' admirable deeds and inspiring accomplishments.

Yet, even as our children's voices are increasingly heard and honored, parent voice (perceived as noise to many children) often garners eye rolls and under-their-breath mutters, backed by the thought that parents just don't get it! Children forget that their parents were children once, too. Parental noise can be in discord with the voices their children welcome. Parents' "irritating" noises are often overshadowed by the "pleasant" sound of video games, Netflix, and tweets. Parent noise often drones on about daily directions, repeated reminders, simple suggestions, and continual do's and don'ts. While some types of parent noise are unquestionably necessary, this must be distinguished from parent voice. In order for parents to gain meaningful airtime, parents must support their children's voices and simultaneously serve as models for how to use voice effectively with others. Only then will our children tune out the noise and tune in to parent voice.

Parent voice and children's voice are characterized as having the ability to speak openly and honestly in an environment that is driven by trust and responsibility. Parents with voice take the time to understand their child's perspective, support their child, *and* advocate together for their child. When you value voice for yourself, you must support the voice of others in your life, and it is about much more than being vocal.

Parent voice is not about volume or control. It is not achieved by shouting or making decisions *for* children. Talking louder does not result in words having more meaning, influence, or value. Voice is a process that encourages parents to *listen* intently to their children, *learn* from them, and *lead together* to support their children's aspirations.

TURN DOWN PARENT NOISE	TURN UP PARENT VOICE
Reduce the number of demands and commands.	Increase explanations for the *why* behind directions or requests.
Reduce emphasis on your opinions.	Increase requests for your children's opinions.
Reduce judgment about others' thoughts and actions.	Increase openness to your children's perspectives and ideas.
Reduce reliance on "parents always know best."	Increase recognition that parents can learn from their children.
Reduce jumping to conclusions before listening.	Increase trust in your children's perspectives.

Getting children to tune in to parent voice requires a conscious effort and practice by parents; it requires careful consideration about how and when you interact with your children on a daily basis. What opportunities are there to build the necessary trust and responsibility for voice to flourish for both parents and children? The opportunities do not need to be extravagant, just reliable—it is the everyday moments that matter: reading a bedtime story, having a snack together, acknowledging your child's hard work at school, playing a game, walking to school, or appreciating your child's assistance with younger siblings. Your children will know that this is a time when they have your attention. And you theirs. When life gets hectic, or school and work schedules conflict, even leaving notes for each other builds trust and a form of communication. When communication and time together are routine, raising any issue, large or small, is less daunting for children, and they can rely on these opportunities to discuss what is on their minds. Even when they choose not to share, relationships are fostered, as the shared experiences help everyone involved get to know each other a little better.

And for the times when in-person interactions are not an option, there is always. . . .

THE NEW LANGUAGE

Texting has firmly secured its place in today's society—for better or worse. Let's start with the drawbacks. Texting allows us to be somewhat lazy and, in an ironic way, disconnected. Full-sentence, in-person conversations are replaced by abbreviations, acronyms, and emojis. Consider this (actual!) text exchange:

> How r u?
> IDK
>
> What do u want for dinner?
> Watev
>
> Where r u?
> Upstairs
>
> TTYL ☺

Who would have ever thought that the word "you" could become even shorter?! And with the abbreviations, there are the multiple meanings to consider: NP can mean "no problem" or "nosy parents." As far as being lazy goes, have you ever found yourself texting your child . . . when they are only as far away as another room? We have!

While texting can seem distant and disconnected in some ways, it is an incredibly convenient way to stay connected. It is great for coordinating logistics and a good conversation starter for someone who may be shy in person. For parents whose work takes them away in the evenings, who travel for weeks, or are away for months at a time, texting is an invaluable way to continually let children know you are thinking about them. In addition to its convenience, texting is powerful because it is in our children's wheelhouse. While we may not be able to keep up with their ever-evolving texting language and, by the way (BTW) ("Mom, you don't need to spell the entire word!"), using the medium they are so comfortable with increases your opportunities to connect.

No matter where texting falls on your preference scale, it is still important to have live conversations, for those conversations provide cues through tone of voice and body language that are important for interpreting emotions in a conversation. For many parents, including ourselves, "live" includes Skype and Facetime. Remember to periodically ask yourself:

- Have I recently paid attention to the expression on my child's face during a discussion? (Emojis do not count.)

- What was the last thing I discussed in person, on the phone, or through video chat with my child? What did his tone of voice tell me?

- Have I recently walked into the other room to start a conversation instead of texting my child?

Texts undoubtedly have a place in communication, but live conversations still matter. TMWFI (Take my word for it!). Modeling voice and supporting children's voices requires parents to engage in real conversations. Next time you pick up your phone to text your child, consider talking instead. And think about how tone of voice, facial expressions, and/or body language impact your understanding of the conversation, your child's mood, etc.

The Responsibility of Voice

Getting our children to tune in—in person and via text—is only the first step. Voice has unlimited potential at home, at school, and in life. And it comes with responsibilities for both parents and children.

First, there is personal responsibility for voice. "What I say and the choices I make are a reflection of who I am." Parents and children must be able to reconcile their words and actions with the type of person they want to be. If I state a strong opinion, assert myself, or even go against a stated norm, is that okay with me? Will I have a sleepless night rethinking what I said, or will I be proud that I stood up for my beliefs?

There are rewards and consequences for what we say and do. Part of personal responsibility is taking ownership of both; it is about taking positive action when you know you can make a difference and making amends when mistakes are made. When a child says "I am sorry" because he truly feels remorse (rather than because a parent told him to say it), he is accepting personal responsibility.

"Think before you speak" is a productive adage to abide by, for both parents and children. Developing responsibility, for intended as well as unintended consequences associated with your own voice, builds both character and integrity. Ultimately, our children have to be responsible to themselves and for themselves. They will not always have parents, teachers, or siblings telling them what to do and when to do it.

Those who seek a voice in matters at home, school, work, or society also need to understand that with voice comes a responsibility toward others. This type of responsibility involves realizing that voice has power beyond oneself and the opportunity to take action. We have all experienced friends, colleagues, and community members who spout rhetoric, make campaign promises, and ramble on about how they were wronged. One might think, "Wow, they have a strong voice!" Not necessarily. They may be effective orators, but stating an opinion or demanding change without the intent to participate in the process is not the kind of voice we are talking about. Proclamations and complaints are meaningless unless they are accompanied by a sense of responsibility and action. How often do you hear people claim to support environmental causes, yet drink bottled water? Or people complain about the local school board but never attend a meeting or vote for school board members at election time? What about parents who are frustrated with their local schools but, rather than become involved and take action toward improvement, choose to berate the school staff in the grocery store? *Without responsibility and action, voice is simply sound.* As you read about ways to listen, learn, and lead to foster voice, keep in mind that a responsible use of voice ultimately leads to positive action and change.

Mom's Musings on Voice

As the mother (KF) of a formally shy child, I used to worry about my child's lack of participation in the classroom. How would she share her thoughts and ideas, her voice? Would she get overlooked? Bullied? How was she going to express herself?

I recall my first introduction to how parents view voice. It was during a parent/child music class when my daughter was about three years old. I am practically tone deaf, and I hoped that by enrolling my child in an early music program, she would have some semblance of a chance to distinguish between the F and C on a scale.

While all the other children in the class where running around, singing, and playing instruments, my child sat clinging to me for dear life. The volume and chaotic nature of the class were not comfortable for her. One of the parents of a particularly loud child remarked, "Oh isn't that cute! You must be a stay-at-home mom. Your child will surely come out of her shell in first grade." I replied, "My child goes to day care. Why does she need to be loud? Maybe your kid should be quiet for once!" Okay, I did not actually say that, but I thought it! Instead, I just smiled and nodded. Secretly, I did want my daughter to break free of me, ask questions, and join in the chaos.

My child never did participate in the music class (and dare I say she is as tone deaf as me!). She continued to be shy throughout elementary school. However, I stopped fretting about it. I realized that there is nothing wrong with a child who is quiet or shy. I came to understand that voice is not about being brash or outgoing. Not every child likes loud noises, chaos, or new settings. A loud child can be as voiceless as a quiet child. Voice is not about volume. Children can express their voices through their actions and involvement, using minimal words. I learned that forcing a child to speak up is not always the best way to foster voice. That morning in music class broadened my understanding of voice. It made me more prepared to support my child in developing her own voice, in her own way. And I am now more prepared to advocate for just that!

Schools can tend to reward the vocal students. The classroom is designed for students to speak up, express themselves, and share out loud. It is important that children are provided opportunities to have quiet time and are not always required to share verbally. Shy is but one characteristic of a person; it does not define the person. And it certainly does not indicate the value of his voice, or its effectiveness. (Of course, now that I have a "loud" teenager, I long for those quiet, peaceful moments when my child was shy!)

Lesson Learned: *Use your voice to challenge preconceived ideas of voice. Celebrate quiet, introverted children and the different ways they express their voices.*

Dad's Deliberations on Voice

I (RQ) am fortunate enough to travel around the world, sharing what I believe makes a difference for kids. Whenever possible, I bring one of my children with me. I want them to broaden their horizons, develop their own aspirations, and make a difference in the world.

One of my daughters attended a conference where I was the keynote speaker. I wanted to go check out the conference center the evening before and asked her to come with me. We walked into the grand ballroom. Upon seeing 3,000 chairs set up, she immediately asked with incredible excitement, "Who is speaking here?" I proudly replied, "I am." She laughed and said, "Seriously, Dad, who is speaking here?" She was shocked—even disbelieving. I had to walk her over to a poster displaying my picture and the location of my keynote—the grand ballroom.

The next morning, I could tell she was incredibly nervous. She was not concerned about my actual presentation or how well it would go; rather, she was very concerned that no one would show up! I didn't admit to her that I worry about that myself sometimes! Fortunately, her concerns were allayed. People did indeed show up, even to the point of standing room only. My presentation was well received, prompting a standing ovation. I was so proud, especially since my daughter, who originally feared I'd be presenting to empty seats, was there. I could not wait to see her and hear her thoughts.

When we finally reconnected, I asked her in an admittedly proud-peacockish manner, "So, what did you think of that?" I was anticipating, "Awesome!", "You were amazing!", or "I loved it!" Instead, she offered, "I really don't get it. Why were people so excited when all you talk about is common sense things that everyone already knows?" I did not know how to respond. I was honestly a little crushed but tried to respond in a nonchalant, let-it-roll-off-my-back kind of way. Once I fully absorbed her feedback (it took some time!), I embraced the learning.

Since that time almost 10 years ago, I prepare for every single presentation with my daughter's perspective as an audience member in mind. I am hypersensitive to not talking about the obvious. Instead, I strive to push people's thinking to another level and offer something new every time. My daughter challenged me to be a much better presenter, literally by using her voice. Her feedback was effective because she was honest, and I was willing to listen, albeit while swallowing my pride!

Lesson Learned: *We are not always prepared for what another voice will reveal, but we should always remain willing to learn from it.*

REFLECT ON VOICE

- *Think about your experiences with voice as a child. Would you put your parents in the noise or voice category? Consider how your experiences impact your beliefs about voice as a parent.*

- *When do you find yourself being background noise to your children?*

- *How do you teach your children to appropriately use their voices at home and school?*

TUNING INTO YOUR OWN VOICE

We have all made resolutions that just do not stick. New Year's Day is famous for that. Make this a resolution you keep: Turn down the noise and use your voice in a way that makes your children want to tune in. Start by assessing your own actions related to voice. How do you score yourself?

1	2	3	4	5
Never	Rarely	Sometimes	Usually	Always

SCORE

I demonstrate to my child that I believe I can learn a lot from him.	_____
I regularly ask for my child's thoughts and opinions.	_____
I show my child I respect his ideas and perspectives.	_____
I listen intently to my child.	_____
I use my voice as a positive force for change.	_____
I take responsibility for my voice and choices.	_____
I am aware of the volume and tone of my voice when speaking with my child.	_____
I communicate honestly and openly with my child.	_____
I involve my child in age-appropriate decision making.	_____
I encourage my child to use his voice effectively.	_____

Obviously on any given day, parents might score themselves differently. Every parent experiences the feelings of being overwhelmed, over stressed, and over questioned! There is no average score for the above statements; rather, they are simply designed to cause parents to pause and consider their current actions related to voice and hopefully strive to change scores on the statements that matter the most to them and their children.

In addition, families interact in unique ways for various reasons, be it personalities, culture, or life circumstances. While RQ's Italian heritage seems to require (very) loud voices to communicate, other families may struggle with helping a child understand that you do not have to be an extrovert to have your voice heard; talking nonstop is not the same as having a voice. Regardless of your voice challenges, the most important starting place is to understand the difference between noise and voice.

Now Hear This!

Even in the moments when parents feel invisible, like they are losing the battle for airtime in their children's lives, it is important to keep in mind that parents' words and actions are noticed more often than they are acknowledged. Yes, even when a child's head remains buried in a book or their eyes remain glued to the screen on their phone, they are noticing. That is reassuring, but it may be time to tip the scales. Think about the balance of noise and voice in your home and remember that it is never too late to turn down parent noise and turn up parent voice.

CHAPTER 2

Listen

Hearing the Right Notes

When people talk, listen completely. Most people never listen.

—Ernest Hemingway

At the end of parent seminars, we always ask for comments and questions. The responses range from thought provoking to YIKES, did he just ask what I think he asked? The latter category leaves us scratching our heads a bit: "My son doesn't like any of his teachers. What is wrong with all of them?" "We have one kid; do you think we should have another?" "Our oldest child never listens to us. Is it because he has red hair?" (All questions that were actually asked!)

We also have our own YIKES moments all the time, including things that cannot possibly be followed through on. For example, I (RQ) once confidently proclaimed: "Sit still or I am going to take you off the plane this second!" That would have been quite an accomplishment, seeing as we had been airborne for about 30 minutes. On a different trip, I heard a father yell at his kid to "Stop crying or I'll give you something to cry about!" A classic line heard many times before but never really thought about that deeply . . . until this child's response: "I don't need something else to cry about, I am already crying!" How can we expect our kids to listen to us when the things we say, especially during moments of frustration, do not make sense to them? Consider the classic, "If your head was not attached, you would probably lose it." For real?

The challenge of being listened to is not just a parent concern but also a child concern. Throughout the course of our work in schools, children have told us that they feel their parents do not truly listen to them. While children feel their thoughts and ideas are too easily dismissed, on the flip side, the parents feel tuned out. The takeaway here is that parents and children need to listen *completely* to each other. Easy, right? Well, only on the surface. . .

Listening can appear to be an easy task. Sounds are all around us all the time. Listening to the sounds does not create any type of physical strain on the body. In fact, people often overhear things when they are not even trying. But listening is not that straightforward, and listening is not always an auditory task. Individuals with hearing, speech, or language disorders use other means of communication, including sign language, lipreading, and assistive technology. Vocal chords are not the only means of communication, and true listening involves more than simply hearing, reading lips, or knowing sign language; it requires a conscious effort—a focus and desire to understand what someone else is communicating. Sometimes listening completely takes more concentration than other times. For instance, the YIKES questions require you to look behind the wording to get at the core of the question. Listening completely always involves being fully present.

There are times when I (RQ) am talking with one of my children, making direct eye contact, and I will be told with a less-than-happy tone, "You are not even listening!" And sometimes they are right. I always *hear* them, but I am not always *listening*. I have come to realize that listening is an incredibly intentional activity. It requires more than being physically present; it requires a conscious effort to focus on what is being said. There is nothing passive about it.

Have you ever agreed to your child's request and realized later that you have no idea what you agreed to? While kids cannot seem to remember where to put the dirty laundry, where the dishwasher is, or where they left their phone, they have steel trap memories when it comes to what their parents promised they would do. And they have a knack for securing these promises while their parents are in the midst of a state of disengagement.

The mind is amazing—infinitely capable, yet at the same time the very thing that can interfere with truly listening. The mind allows us to multitask, which is great if you are doing laundry and watching the news, but not so great if you are listening to your child and simultaneously coordinating the day's errands in your mind. Truly listening requires an effort to stay focused on the people with whom we are conversing and engaged with the topic at hand. It is being present in the moment and engaging our mind, not just our ears, in the conversation. While this is admittedly more difficult when one is tired or not interested in a particular topic, it does not make listening at those times less important. It just requires more effort.

Parents (everyone, really, especially in today's age of technology) must practice listening. Yes, we said it—*practice* listening. There are so many distractions in today's world—so many to do's and so much available at our fingertips—that parents (and children) must consciously stop and give their full attention to the current conversation. Sure, some multitasking will occur, because the dishes and laundry will always be whispering at us, and certainly our children's more straightforward questions "What's for dinner?" "Am I at mom or dad's house this weekend?" "Can I play one more video game?" can be answered at the same time. But more meaningful discussions such as "I am starting to feel left out by my friends," "I am feeling overwhelmed in science class," "Can we get a pet rat?" require focus and full attention—from everyone involved. And certainly there is a continuum for the types of questions, as well as the demands on parents, that impact their ability to fully engage on a moment's notice. Time and life are always moving forward, but if the effort is made to really listen the best we can at a given moment, then what parents learn will amaze them and how children feel will be amazing. When you listen completely, those involved feel valued and validated.

LISTENING MATTERS

Listening falls under the "Of course I . . ." umbrella, as does so much of what parents do for their children. *Of course I* take care of my kids when they are sick, *of course I* remind them to wear a hat in the winter and boots in the rain, *of course I* listen to them. Parents may not consciously think about listening; they just do it. But the question is—how effectively? Listening is more than being there, asking a few questions, and nodding your head. Mindless head nods take little effort, engagement, or even thought. And those passive nods can lead to promises to which we never intended to agree. More dessert, new Amazon purchases, extra TV time, a ride to the mall, skipping school. Listening is an active process, and children can most certainly distinguish when they are truly being listened to and when they are simply receiving the multitasking nod. While they may even be happier with the latter on occasion, "YES! I can have more ice cream/buy another video game/watch another show/shop instead of going to school," they do not want to be dismissed on more significant topics. Effective listening builds respect and trust, and contributes to fostering children's self-confidence. It gives them the immensely important message that *they matter*, as do their opinions, thoughts, and ideas, even when they differ from those of their parents. Hence, the importance of practice, no matter your interest level in a particular topic.

Who hasn't gritted their teeth at one time or another to get through a child's discussion, presentation, or activity? Children's interests may not always align with their parents'. Maybe dinosaurs, Comic-Con, video games, or a particular sport is not your thing, but it is your child's latest passion. That is when listening needs to kick into high gear! It is important to show an interest in your children's interests, even when they don't align with your passions. It is also great to become involved when you can. You do not need to be able do a slam dunk or know the latest dance move, you just need to participate in the activities with your children at the level you can. There are ways to stay connected when that participation cannot be in person. In addition to the traditional phone call, we have seen parents use technology to engage with their children, from live video chats to apps that allow distant read alouds or collaborative drawing to creating videos of themselves trying the latest dance move gone viral. The shared experiences and time spent together show you are interested in learning about what they care about. Really, at the end of the day, it is about how it makes your children feel. You don't need to be an expert; you just need to be interested. Listening demonstrates to children that you care about them, their ideas, and your relationship. This is true for children of all ages. Whether it is about the latest toddler toy, a new teenage band, or the newest app, children want to share their interests and be listened to. Parents' ability to listen and become involved not only helps build strong, respectful relationships between parent and child but also influences how children interact with others.

Parents are models of behavior for their children. The way parents listen teaches children how to listen to others. Half-heartedly listening teaches children to half listen to others. Listening with judgment or responding with hurtful sarcasm teaches children to be judgmental and sarcastic toward others. Actively listening with the desire to understand, engage, and empathize, on the other hand, models respectful listening and an appreciation for differing interests and points of view.

Keys to Effective Listening

All parents strive to connect with their children. Parents naturally want to know their children and want to support them in becoming themselves. Parents hope and plan to listen to their children. All too often, however, parents promote a "First listen to me, and then (maybe) I will listen to you" approach. Listening is not a competition or a zero-sum game. Rather, it should be a two-way street; a reciprocal process where everyone's thoughts are valued. There are a few ways, however, that adults unintentionally sabotage this. For example, parents may truly listen only when it is convenient for them, too quickly dismiss children's perspectives when they differ from their own, or be tempted to respond with a quick, little white lie for ease. Any of these can result in missing entirely what our children are trying to tell us—a fun story, a sad moment, an inner feeling, an aspiration. Parents may miss an opportunity to connect and understand their children—all because they did not provide their full attention or failed to let their children fully express themselves.

There are several pieces that will help you connect with your children through more effective listening: *Respect*, *Empathy*, *Honesty*, and *Attitude*.

Respect: Active listening simultaneously requires and builds respect. Parents cannot truly listen unless they are willing to respect their children's perspectives and ideas. This does not mean they have to agree with their children; rather, respect involves realizing that people of all ages have different, valid opinions. Children need to know that their ideas do not have to mirror yours. You may like hamburgers and they like hot dogs. You may prefer pets with four legs and fur, but they love reptiles. Although the above examples are simple, we all know that as children age, the differences can become quite stark. Accepting these simple differences shows respect. If children do not think their parents respect their opinions, they will not bother sharing. After all, what's the point? Children will be less likely to engage in conversation and more likely to employ single-word responses, such as "Yah," "Sometimes," or "Whatever."

Respectful listening involves withholding judgmental and sarcastic comments, allowing children to feel safe opening up about their thoughts, ideas, and feelings. Sharing feelings and ideas is a risk, no matter how old you are or how well you know someone. There are times when parents just need to be present and listen, to respect the opinions of their children without inserting their own. Withholding judgment does not mean parents will never provide advice or opinions. It means listening to the child and considering his viewpoint before jumping in. And then, if the situation warrants it, parents will judge and offer advice as necessary. Sarcasm is worth a special note here—many children do not truly grasp sarcasm until high school age, and even then, they do not always appreciate it. Even when a comment is intended as a joke to lighten a mood, it can be interpreted as disrespectful or even mean. Listening respectfully is an essential component of demonstrating to children that their ideas and opinions are valued.

 REFLECT—RESPECT

- *How do you show your children you respect their ideas and opinions?*
- *Think about someone in your life who is a respectful listener. In what ways does this person demonstrate respect during your conversations?*

Empathy: Empathy, as distinguished from sympathy, is probably one of the most undervalued attributes of effective listening. Sympathetic listeners show compassion while listening, whereas empathetic listeners try to put themselves in the other person's shoes. For example, a middle school child may come home and share how stressed he is at school. A parent showing sympathy may express that he feels badly about his son's stress and give him a hug but perhaps not fully consider the impact of the stress from the son's perspective. An empathetic parent considers all the stressors that middle school life can trigger each day, including homework, friendships, fitting in, co-curricular activities, and puberty. The parent recalls what it feels like to be stressed and acknowledges the physical and mental toll it takes. She recognizes that a 12-year-old's stressors are different than an adult's, yet acknowledges that the 12-year-old's experiences are very real. Parents who listen with empathy relate and understand in a manner that allows for validation of their children's experiences and feelings.

REFLECT—EMPATHY

- *What words do you use to show empathy when listening to your child?*

- *Reflect on what it felt like to be the same age as your child is now. What did you worry about? What excited you? What did your parents not understand about you?*

Honesty: Children of all ages can readily detect when a parent is not being honest. When parents share false praise, make insincere comments, or pretend to understand, children know. Children want the same honesty from their parents that their parents expect of them. Of course, there are occasions when the little white lie is warranted. It may be the means to finally getting out the door when your teenage daughter has on an acceptable, even if not your favorite, outfit after changing clothes three times, or it may be to protect a younger child from worrying about an issue they cannot yet fully comprehend (financial concerns, relationships, tragic events on the news, etc.). It is important to keep respect at the core of your comments and conversations.

When children know that a parent's general approach is one of honesty, they, too, feel they can be honest about their own experiences. However, when a child knows his parent is being dishonest, the listening process is undermined. Once someone is dishonest, it is difficult to trust what they say going forward. When we don't, our children begin to question the truth about what they are told. They find themselves in a quandary, deciding, quite literally, whether to listen or not—whether what they are being told by their parents is true or not.

REFLECT—HONESTY

- *How do you model honesty for your children?*
- *How do you let your children know that they can be honest with you, even when their opinions differ from yours?*

Attitude: The word "attitude" often conjures up negativity for parents. By default, people think of attitude as bad, unpleasant, or sarcastic—all of which we could all do without. We believe one's attitude is important and should be reflected in a positive approach toward listening. A positive attitude shows engagement and interest, as compared to being indifferent and disinterested. Attitude moves beyond compliance or passive listening; it is a display of involvement. Parents with a positive attitude actively listen to their children and demonstrate that they *want* to listen to them.

There are moments, for parents and children alike, when negative attitudes enter conversations, reflected in eye rolls, downward stares, and quick quips. It is important to not be pulled into that. Parents must model a positive attitude and make a conscious commitment to ensure their comments, posture, tone of voice, and facial expressions demonstrate that they are listening. Gestures and words display strong attitudes of either "I care" or "I could not care less!"—make it the former.

Consider the scenario of an eight-year-old daughter struggling with the interactions within a group of friends. She shares that her friends are mean and make fun of her. A parent may believe the feud will pass and does not warrant the anxiety it is causing, or the parent's attitude could be one of indifference, advising her daughter to wait it out or "just get over it." A parent could even express an attitude of disappointment with the choices of the other children. Alternately, a parent can truly listen to her daughter and work to understand her perspective and the impact the situation is having on her. The conflict matters greatly *to the child*, even if the parent's perspective differs. The child may not always be right, but she always *has the right* to her perspective and the feelings that accompany it. By listening in a way that honors this, the parent demonstrates an attitude that she cares, is there to support her child, and will help her work through the experience.

 REFLECT—ATTITUDE

- *What attitude do you convey when your child wants to share information with you?*
- *How can you ensure that the attitude you want to convey is what your child is experiencing?*

With listening, like so many skills in life, there is always room for improvement. Practice may not always make perfect, but it does lead to progress. There will certainly be moments when it is easier and more efficient to simply tell your child what to do rather than hear her reasons behind what she wants to do. And yes, there will be moments when you are too exhausted to listen effectively and you will promise something yet have no recollection of it, until your child pulls out her nail polish and says, "Dad, I can't wait to paint your nails bright pink and braid your hair!"

In our increasingly busy daily lives, stopping to listen is not always easy. But it is always important. Even with these four keys—Respect, Empathy, Honesty, and Attitude—practiced and in place, life's daily pace can make it challenging to truly listen. Parents must accept the reality that they cannot always drop everything on a moment's notice to listen; parents have many responsibilities and their schedules are not always conducive to listening *at exactly the right time*. What parents can do, however, is show their children that they consistently do listen *over time*, and that they will always *find the time*.

All kids (teenagers included!) want to be listened to and understood. It is up to parents to create these opportunities and capture these moments whenever they can—and when they do, to listen in a way that shows children that they are heard, that they are respected, and that their opinions and feelings are valued.

Mom's Musings on Listening

When my (KF) oldest daughter came home with a tattoo, my initial reaction was, well, less than receptive. "Do you realize you will have that forever?" "Do you know what that tattoo will look like on wrinkles when you're older?" "How will you get a job?" "What does that even mean?" "Don't you have to be at least 25 to get a tattoo without a parent's permission?" "Did you get funky body piercings as well?" After the initial shock wore off and the guilt over all my parental failings faded, I was able to actually listen to her.

Photo courtesy of Kris Fox

She asked me, "Do you remember when you were a teenager and your friend double pierced your ear in your bathroom?" Ugh. When did I tell her that (true) story? "You said everyone had double-pierced ears. And you only wore your second earring when you left the house. For my generation, tattoos are the double-pierced ears from your day. I love my tattoo." Aside from the fact that I did not know I was so old, maybe she had a point. It was her way of expressing herself, it was an illustration (literally) of the times, and it was her body.

Maybe I just needed to listen rather than immediately judge. Ten years later, my older daughters both have more than one

(Continued)

(Continued)

tattoo, are gainfully employed, happy, well adjusted, and, yes, they both still love their tattoos. Maybe someday I will get a matching tattoo with my granddaughter.

Lesson Learned: My childhood is not my children's childhood. What was "in" many years ago does change. I do not have to agree, but I do need to listen and try to understand.

Dad's Deliberations on Listening

The first time my (RQ) daughter got a tattoo, my immediate reaction was to worry about what *my* father would think. How was I ever going to be able to tell him about *this*? If that does not tell you something about the power of parents, I am not sure what does! I was in my 50s, and the first thing I thought of when my daughter got a tattoo was saving face with my 80-year-old father. (Cute, in a way, but somewhat pathetic at the same time.)

I learned about the tattoo during a phone call, and I am proud to say that I managed to hold my tongue. I am admittedly not a big fan of confrontational calls, as they leave too much space for misconceptions and hurt feelings. I took the "high road" at the time, while still planning to address it in person later, making it clear that I am not a fan of tattoos and was disappointed in her decision. Even though she was over 21, I was still a bit shocked that she did not ask me before obtaining the body art.

The day of in-person reckoning arrived, but before I could jump in with my litany of reasons why tattoos were a bad idea, she walked through the front door proudly displaying her new tattoo. "I could not wait for you to see this! I knew you would love it . . . It's a quail!!!!" Quaglia means quail in Italian. After my daughter's display of complete confidence that I would be so pleased, what was I left to say? I said what any strong-headed Italian would have said, "Wow, that is

(Continued)

(Continued)

incredibly thoughtful and amazing. I love it!" (Until she reads this book, she will still think I love it. And while I do love her pride in it, deep down inside, I do wonder how perky and cute the quail will look when she is 60 years old with perhaps a few more wrinkles on her biceps.)

Lesson Learned: Listen to the whole story before rushing to any judgment. It will demonstrate that you are willing to listen, and it will allow your children to feel comfortable sharing their thoughts, ideas, and experiences. It shows them that you value their opinions and their values.

REFLECT ON LISTENING

- *When and where are you most effective listening to your children? In the evening? During the morning? In the car? At the dinner table?*

- *When and where do you find your children are most apt to talk with you?*

- *How do you vary your listening approach for each of your children? Does one prefer to talk when you are alone while another wants to talk as a family?*

PARENT VOICE

LISTENING: TAKE ACTION

Listening completely is a challenge. Daily life is always beckoning us to multitask, and the "To Do" lists are perpetual. But our children deserve our best, most complete listening. Start by getting their feedback. Ask your child to rate you on the following items, responding with **Always, Sometimes,** or **Never.**

1. I truly listen (no multitasking) when you share your interests and ideas.

2. I listen to your ideas with an open mind.

3. I work with you to solve problems.

4. I demonstrate to you that I value your perspective.

5. I respect when you need space and time to yourself.

Keep in mind that how your child rates you is somewhat fluid. It may be influenced by a recent interaction and reflective of how she is feeling in response to that situation. While it may not always reflect how she would "score" you overall, it is a valid measure of how she is feeling at that time and a great springboard for discussion and action. The following are some strategies to practice being a better listener.

INSTEAD OF ASKING GENERAL QUESTIONS, *TRY BEING SPECIFIC*

Questions that are too open ended may lead to one-word responses. "How was your day?" "Fine." "How did things go at practice today?" "Great." Try asking specific questions that require details when responding, such as, "What is one thing you can teach me from your Spanish class today?" Include questions that allow for children to express the emotions of their experiences: What is one thing that happened today that was funny? At what point of the day were you most frustrated/happy/sad, and why?

INSTEAD OF INSERTING ADVICE, TRY BEING OPEN TO YOUR CHILDREN'S SUGGESTIONS

As parents, our default mode often is to dispense advice or demonstrate our understanding by sharing similar stories from when we were our children's age. Instead of immediately jumping in with solutions or stories, encourage your child to articulate his own thoughts and brainstorm solutions for a situation. For example, a teenager might be struggling with something routine, such as how to complete a project for school, or as intricate as how to stand up to peer pressure. It can be tempting to provide directions on how to approach the project or to share stories about your own teen years and how you responded to challenges with peers. While children appreciate a certain amount of guidance and "I remember when . . ." stories, children can be dismissive of both when provided too frequently. Before providing personal stories or advice, ask your child what he thinks about a situation. Ask him to think through his choices and the consequences and learning that can come from each. Then, if your story is dying to be told, by all means, share it!

INSTEAD OF GRILLING FOR ANSWERS, TRY DISCUSSING IDEAS

Time is a limited resource. While it can be more efficient to "grill" a child for a succinct answer rather than engage in a discussion, the latter is where the real meaning lies. Grilling questions start with Who, What, When, Where, or Did. For example: Who went to the football game with you? What grade did you receive on your test? Did you score any points in your game? Instead of grilling, ask your child questions that require explanations and allow time for conversations and the exchange of ideas. These discussions often don't start with a question at all; they involve statements that start with Tell me, Show me, or Teach me:

- Tell me about the test you took today. Was it easy or hard? Why?

- Show me the best move you made in the game today. How did it impact the game?

- Teach me your new jump rope move. How did you learn it?

Granted, sometimes parents need to ask pointed questions and need a quick, direct reply: "Who are you going to the movie with?" "Where will you be going after?" "What time is your curfew?" Brevity is great for quick, factual information; discussions are great for sharing insights, ideas, and feelings.

INSTEAD OF THINKING "I KNOW BEST," TRY BELIEVING "WE KNOW BEST"

To build trust, children need to know that a conversation is about two people. That means that *both* people deserve airtime. Listening is the antithesis of lecturing; rather, the goal is to create two-way conversations where adults and children *listen to each other* and respectfully share their ideas. To assist in the process, encourage your children to ask you questions. Help everyone involved recognize the importance of respecting differing points of views. More often than not, there are multiple reasonable perspectives on a topic and more than one "best" way to solve an issue. Consider the scenario of a child studying for a test. Many parents often transfer their own work habits onto their child. The parent may work best at a desk, in a silent room, with a break every half hour. But the child may be just the opposite. He may find background music helps him focus, lying on the ground is more comfortable, and working for hours at a time without getting up is no problem. Rather than setting out to determine the single "right" way to approach work habits, have a conversation with your child about why a certain setting or desk (or floor) arrangement works and what the benefits of each are. Talk about the merits and drawbacks of various work habits and recognize that personal preferences apply. You may be surprised by what you learn!

INSTEAD OF FORCING CONVERSATIONS, TRY RESPECTING INTROSPECTION

We live in a culture where people can get airtime all the time—there is an avenue for expressing yourself 24/7. When you add to that the multitude of children's responsibilities and interests (school, work, co-curricular activities, friends), there is little time left for quiet time or down time. Realize that your child may not feel like talking at the same time you do. She is not necessarily being defiant; rather, it might simply be a time when she wants to decompress and think for herself. Respect the need for children to have some quiet time and work to find an alternate time for conversation.

INSTEAD OF FORMING JUDGMENTS, TRY TRUSTING YOUR CHILD'S PERSPECTIVE

As children form their own opinions and ideas, parents can too readily judge and presume their children's lack of experience detracts from the strength of their perspective. Parents' ability to listen to and accept the views their children express is important. These views will change myriad times over the years and sometimes within the course of a single day. However, children need to know that their opinions are valued, even when they differ from the opinions of their parents. When my son voted for the first time, I was shocked to learn that he voted in a manner quite the opposite from his family. I impulsively presumed this was due to his lack of experience with voting and not fully understanding the issues; he must have voted that way because his friends voted one way or he just wanted to take the opposite stance from his parents. Then I stopped to consider it more. I halted the judgement and talked to him. After hearing his reasons, I realized that he knew exactly why he voted the way he did and felt strongly about his positions. While I didn't agree, I was able to step back and be proud that he voted, informed and with conviction.

As you consider these strategies and reflect on how your children rated your listening skills, keep track of when you and your children truly listen best. What time of day is most effective? For some parents, listening after 9 p.m. is not realistic. The homework assignment the child wants checked at 10 p.m.? Not happening—parent is half asleep. While for other parents, any listening before a first, or even second, cup of coffee is not realistic. What they hear about their child's day as they are getting out of bed does not stick in the memory bank. All three children want to talk with you at the same time? Not possible, you are only one person. Where are your children most engaged in conversation? Some children listen best when they are in the car, going to and from school or various activities. Others listen best and engage more during the dinner hour. Knowing when you and your children listen best can help everyone find the most effective times to engage in meaningful conversations.

Listening takes time and practice. Most parents do not naturally listen completely. There are many distractions in today's society that constantly call for our attention, and we sometimes want to immediately dispense advice instead of listening fully to the other person's situation and perspective. Becoming a skilled listener requires effort and a desire to truly hear what children have to say.

Listening Through the Years

This section presents ideas to help parents better understand and practice effective listening with children at various ages. As with all developmental recommendations, keep in mind that not all children fit neatly into their age category. Consider which descriptors best suit your child and follow the recommendations for that age range.

4- to 7-Year-Olds

Seem to Have a Short Attention Span

- Eliminate surrounding noise and distractions when possible.
- Recognize the time of day when your child is tired and just needs quiet time.

Love Asking Questions

- Provide opportunities every day for your child to ask questions.
- Ask your child open-ended questions to engage in dialogue and discover answers together.

Misinterpret Body Language

- Be expressive when you talk.
- Role-play with your child and discuss how to interpret various facial expressions (e.g., angry, sad, happy).

Use Limited Vocabulary

- Provide some word choices as options for your child ("Are you angry or sad about something?").

- Demonstrate different ways your child can express her thoughts and emotions (e.g., verbally, artistically, or through dramatic play).

8- to 10-Year-Olds

Direction Overload

- Build in some quiet time for children to think.

- Ensure there are opportunities for your children to make their own choices.

Strong Sense of Right and Wrong

- Take the time to explain why certain decisions are made and why you think they are fair.

- Ask children to help you develop fair resolutions to situations in which they find themselves (e.g., how to share toys with friends, amount of time they can use electronics).

Argue Before Listening

- Help your child understand that there are various perspectives on issues. Select a scenario he is familiar with and talk about both sides of the situation.

- Let your child state his point first sometimes, and then other times you start the discussion with your point of view.

(Continued)

(Continued)

Sensitive to Criticism

- Encourage your children to share their emotions and reactions to various events; use this to lead discussions, maintaining an awareness of your child's sensitivity.

- Celebrate the various strengths of your child. Think outside of the academic context: What decisions does she make socially? Is she kind to others? Does she challenge herself to try new things?

11- to 13-Year-Olds

Believe Parents Know Nothing
("You just don't understand!")

- Balance providing advice with simply listening to your child; show you understand that being a teenager today is in many ways different than when you were a teenager.

- Summarize what you heard back to your child to ensure you understood what he meant.

Fear Failure

- Listen to your children's concerns about failure and not doing well enough. This is a great opportunity for parents to assuage those fears and talk about how everyone experiences failure and that it can be a productive way to learn.

- Respond to failure with guidance and support, rather than anger and frustration.

Desire Independent Decision-making Opportunities

- Provide your teenager with choices so that he can make decisions (which you may agree with or not!).

- Discuss ethical dilemmas and debatable issues with your child.

Increased Importance of Peer Group

- Give your preteens space with friends, yet continue dialogue with them about having the confidence to make decisions that are right for them.
- Celebrate your children's positive friends.

14- to 18-Year-Olds

Friends' Voices Have Increased Influence

- Ask your child about her friends and learn about their interests, hopes, and dreams.
- Do not compete; rather, help your teenager sort through different pieces of advice and perspectives, ultimately developing responsibility for their own voice.

Autonomy

- Recognize that independence is a positive part of growing up.
- Remember, teenagers need to practice making decisions. After all, how can you teach someone responsibility if they are never given the opportunity to be responsible?

Crave a Good Debate

- Talk with your teenager about current events and life issues that are relevant to her.
- Play devil's advocate when appropriate to help your teenager see the other side of an issue.

Desire Space and To Be Left Alone

- Alone time is not a bad thing. Give your child space when he needs it.
- Respect privacy and develop boundaries together.

In Their Own Words: Advice on Listening, from Children to Parents

In our professional roles, we are fortunate to have opportunities to speak with thousands of students each year, from preschool students through high school seniors. Some students come from privileged backgrounds, while others struggle to make it to school after taking care of their siblings. Some students live with their families, while others struggle in and out of foster care. Some students are learning English as a second language, while others are more well-read than all of us combined. From their varied backgrounds, we gain invaluable insights by listening to their experiences and perspectives. We believe that all parents can learn a lot from their children by simply listening. To honor the voice of children, we asked a few to share their advice to parents on how to listen effectively to kids like them.

How to Listen to a Kid Like Me

Nate, age 13

I am humorous and I like to be a leader. The best ways to listen to a kid like me are:

- Don't lecture, *because I usually tune out.*
- Don't be too strict, *because kids need to feel loved.*
- Be caring, *because it makes kids feel noticed.*
- Don't yell, *because I listen better to a calm voice.*
- Be helpful, *because every kid needs support.*

- Be positive, *because if you are negative, your child will reflect that attitude.*

- Inspire your child, *because kids need to feel like their parents care about their future.*

- Most importantly, if there is a problem, speak about it and give your child support **because this is when they will really listen.**

Thomas, age 11

I have Attention Deficit Disorder (ADD). It is not bad. It just means I have to take medicine to slow my brain down. A good thing about ADD is that you are unique. I look at the world differently. The bad thing is that I get in trouble and I don't always think straight.

These are tips to help you listen to your kids. I like to call them:

The Three Ears to Success

1. Just listen to kids. If you see your kid is sad or struggling, just sit them down and really listen.

2. DON'T INTERRUPT. Never interrupt a kid. They either forget what they have to say or feel unimportant.

3. And last, but not least, a parent should show that they are listening. Kids know when parents are not listening. Yes, it is shocking, but it's true. So a parent should make eye contact, make it a major priority to show that they are listening, and wait to give advice until the kids are done sharing.

(Continued)

(Continued)

Audrey, age 15

I love to read and travel. I lived the first 12 years of my life in France and adore stinky cheeses.

To parents,

It is not simple for me to voice my thoughts or start an argument about something important. I usually ignore a problem until it cannot be ignored any longer. I don't necessarily talk about my day or initiate a conversation as much as I should, but there is still a lot I can teach you. The rule is: You can only learn from me if you are willing to listen. So notice the small things, my quirks, and flaws; take all you want from them, they are there so you can learn what kind of person I am. Please do not restrain me or yourself by telling me how to think. Give me room to expand my opinions on my own. Let's argue: Teach me what you know, and I'll tell you what I have learned. We are not in opposition, we are in balance. You and I, it's not going to be easy, but I promise to challenge my beliefs. I truly hope you have the courage to accept them and learn from them. Do not feel like it is only your role to teach me about life. I have a lot to teach you as well. But I will always be there to listen to you, and learn a thing or two, as long as you are there to listen to me.

Love,

The Kid

LISTENING FOR LIFE

When parents welcome home their newborn baby, they listen intently all the time for cues and respond accordingly—a cry means I am hungry, I have some built-up gas, or my diaper needs to be changed. When the crying stops, we feel good as a parent and carry on. Yet as the child gets older and progresses from cries to words, we sometimes listen a little less. How ironic, considering that the older a child becomes, the more she has to say. Why do we listen to newborns more intently than we listen to older children? The answer is straightforward: It is easy to deal with the newborn. We are fully aware that most mothers of newborns will not agree with us right now, but hear us out. The possible responses to newborns are defined, direct, and have an immediate impact on the situation. Once our children start to talk and express themselves differently, we need to listen and respond differently. The topics and responses can be more complex than food and dirty diapers. Our older children may not be crying audibly for tangible things, but they are looking for our attention. Children have a lot to say, and we, in turn, have a lot to learn from them.

Our children deserve nothing less than our best listening. Maya Angelou once said, "People will forget what you said; people will forget what you did; but people will never forget how you made them feel." With our kids, that is true from infancy through adolescence and right into adulthood; it is just how we approach this that changes over time. Truly listening to your children, in different ways at different ages, helps ensure that they feel genuinely respected, trusted, and responsible. It lets them know they matter—a feeling that will last a lifetime.

CHAPTER 3

Learn

Getting in Rhythm

Tell me and I forget. Teach me and I remember. Involve me and I learn.

—Benjamin Franklin

I (RQ) experienced mindless listening (no learning) when my son Casey was in college. Casey was an excellent long-distance runner. He went to school in New York, and one season the track team had a meet at the University of Maine, close to where we lived. We were incredibly excited not only to see our son compete, but I thought it would be awesome to have the team over for dinner. Enthusiasm is great, but mine reached the point of *tuning out*. Casey must have said a hundred times, "Sounds awesome, but I don't think it is a good idea because there are a lot of us on the team and each one eats way more than I do." I laughed and said, "Not to worry, I know how to cook!" Casey reemphasized his point, "Dad, these kids eat like crazy, especially when the food is good and it's the night before a meet." I naively replied, "Great! Even better. I'll cook a lot!"

Photo courtesy of Russ Quaglia

After a week of preparation, the big dinner was finally here. We were so prepared for the team's arrival . . . or so we thought. As the athletes stepped off the buses (yes, plural—two busloads), my first thought was BIG. Have you ever seen a Division 1 college shot putter? My second thought was ". . . and I think Casey may have mentioned something about hungry. . . ." Sure enough, as soon as they entered the front door, they hit the food. I never realized anybody could pile food so high on a plate, never mind eat it all and then load it up again for seconds! I quickly realized we were in trouble. Simply not enough food. Fortunately, we had a freezer in the basement full of, well, I guess you could call it food. This was the kind of food you would only eat if there were a natural disaster and it was the only food left. Well, this was a natural disaster of sorts.

We started defrosting unidentified food and grilling up random meat, hoping to erase any freezer burn. Food panic, for sure. We could not get the food out fast enough for the second wave of the eating frenzy. After what felt like the longest three hours of my life, and with literally NO food left in the house, the team appeared full.

Casey, the team, and the coaches loved the home-cooked experience instead of the typical fast food on road trips, and they thanked us profusely. One coach said, "I hope Casey told you how much these kids eat." I said, "He sure did!" Yes, he did tell me, and I politely listened but failed to truly hear or learn a word from it. Casey could not have been clearer letting me know his teammates eat like it is their last meal. If I had listened to *and* learned from my son, the evening would have been much less stressful. And the runners coming around for a second helping would not have been served microwave-defrosted burritos on the grill . . . or at least that's what I think they were.

Even with the best intentions, parents can get caught in a state of "mindless" listening. It is one thing for this to occur when you need to multitask and the topic is straightforward, such as putting away the breakfast dishes and simultaneously confirming pick-up and drop-off logistics for the day with your child. But it is a completely different experience when your child is trying to share her thoughts or feelings and you are not fully tuned in. Our children deserve our undivided attention for these discussions. When we fail to listen completely, we miss important opportunities to learn about and from them.

Learning Matters

By now, the phrase "lifelong learning" is part of everyday language. In fact, school mission statements appear misguided if this phrase is not included. Companies aspire to hire lifelong learners. However, learning does not just automatically happen. Just because someone reads a book, receives an "A" on a test, or watches a DIY video, it does not mean that learning has occurred. How many times have you read something, only to have to reread it repeatedly in order to understand it? Do you recall a test you took in school when you did not understand the material, but you were able to memorize enough to get by? Have you ever made the same silly mistake more than once? Where is the meaningful learning?

Learning occurs when there is some type of *change*. It may be a change in knowledge, perspective, or experience. The change should cause you to think, pause, and perhaps do something differently. Students learn in school when they gain new knowledge or skills or create something new. Sitting in a classroom does not guarantee learning. If a parent listens passively to his son and does not take in the information, gain insight or understanding, or consider a different viewpoint, there is no learning. Head nodding or pat responses such as "Good job" are acknowledgment but not learning. The time spent listening to our children is most valuable when we learn from them—their ideas, interests, opinions, and aspirations. Everything we learn gives us additional insight into who they are and who they are becoming.

Listening without learning is like eating without the nutritional value. Think about all the occasions when adults ask questions yet are not necessarily interested in the answer. There are the customary niceties: "How are you doing?" "How's the weather?" "What are you doing this weekend?" When asked in passing, these are cordial interactions. However, parents need to go deeper than niceties with their children. Parents must listen with a *sincere* desire to learn. Learning with sincerity includes asking follow-up questions, seeking clarity when unsure, and restating information to confirm understanding. When parents learn from and with their children, they gain insight into their children's perspectives and ideas. A change occurs—awareness of a new interest of their child's, recognition of their child's developing personality, or insight into a different perspective. The possibilities are endless, but we must be mindful to learn while listening rather than mindlessly listen.

MINDFUL LEARNING

Mindful learning involves being inquisitive and demonstrating a willingness to learn from your children. It is easy to be lured into thinking you are learning when you ask your child, "Did you have a good day?" "Did you finish the assignment?" "Was lunch fun?" These are default conversation starters that require minimal effort and a one-word response. These questions lead to learning about basic facts or logistical details. Mindful learning requires engaging in conversations that cannot be answered with a "yes, no, maybe" response. To learn from, about, and with their kids, parents need to engage them in more meaningful conversations.

Mindful learning also requires parents to truly believe that their child has something to teach them. When you demonstrate a willingness to learn from your child, whether about their feelings, perspective, or a new hobby, trust is established. This leads to children realizing that it is okay to have different opinions from their parents. When trust is absent, it is difficult for children to share when they are struggling, such as failing a class or being bullied at school. With trust established, children have confidence that when their parents learn about less-than-stellar decisions, they won't jump straight to judgment or "I told you so" without really listening and learning. Children need to trust that their parents realize they do not know everything and that at least a few things have changed since they were kids. Why, after all, should children try to explain their ideas, experiences, and insights, if their parents already think they know it all or know it better?

Mindful learning takes time and effort. And it is well worth it. This type of interaction encourages voice and thought *from* your children. First, they must truly listen to parents in order to respond with more than a one-word reply (and without their devices in their hand!). Second, they must participate in two-way dialogue to answer questions and engage in meaningful conversations.

LEARNING AND INTERESTS

Children's interests, passions, and unique characteristics are a great starting point for learning. Children of all ages want to engage with others about things that are interesting to them. Hobbies may include Raspberry Pi (hint: it has nothing to do with food), lock picking (really, this is a fun hobby for kids who like puzzles), parkour (caution: we do not recommend adults try this without stretching and some training!), or Dungeons & Dragons. When parents take an interest in their children's interests, a connection emerges. This connection allows parents to show that they care about what their child cares about, are willing to learn from him, and want to spend time with him. No matter how common or obscure the hobby, no matter if you enjoy it or not, if it interests your child, it needs to interest you. Really, how much did you like playing Pokémon?

It is great to share your interests with your children, as well. The goal is to create opportunities for shared experiences where you learn together:

- *Involve* your children in your hobbies and let them discover what you find so interesting.

- *Be prepared* for your child to display less enthusiasm than you. She may not like running or gardening or going to museums.

- *Be aware* of your child's responses and adjust plans accordingly. A half hour at the museum or on the tennis court may be more than enough of an introduction.

Yes, there is a bit of a double standard here. You need to be interested in your child's interests, whether they align with your passions or not. But the reverse may not necessarily be true or worth forcing.

SPEAKING THEIR LANGUAGE

Let's face it, texting is here to stay. While texting can seem brief and superficial, there is actually a great deal that can be learned. Texts are more than a means to pass on trivial information. We just need to read between the lines. And we need to keep in mind that texting matters to kids of all ages. A preschool teacher shared a story with us. One of her four-year-old students said, "Ms. B., next time you are absent, would you please text me?" The teacher replied, "Sweetie, I would love to, but you don't even have a phone!"

On the following page, consider the texts that parents shared with us—all exchanges with their kids.

What can be learned from these texts? Well, aside from noticing that punctuation is optional, many of these texts reflect how the children are feeling (bored, relaxed, optimistic) or what is on their minds (fishing or boys) or a need to be met (feeding a hungry cat or locating a missing bird). Each text is an opportunity to dig deeper and find out more from your child: Why is this class not engaging for you? How could school be made

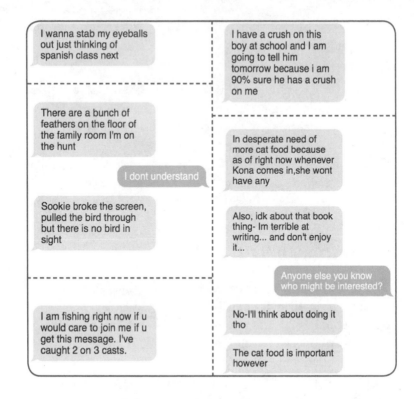

I wanna stab my eyeballs out just thinking of spanish class next

There are a bunch of feathers on the floor of the family room I'm on the hunt

I dont understand

Sookie broke the screen, pulled the bird through but there is no bird in sight

I am fishing right now if u would care to join me if u get this message. I've caught 2 on 3 casts.

I have a crush on this boy at school and I am going to tell him tomorrow because i am 90% sure he has a crush on me

In desperate need of more cat food because as of right now whenever Kona comes in,she wont have any

Also, idk about that book thing- Im terrible at writing... and don't enjoy it...

Anyone else you know who might be interested?

No-I'll think about doing it tho

The cat food is important however

more interesting? Why do you enjoy fishing so much—is it the challenge of catching a fish, the setting, or both? While the "stabbing" text is a bit over the top, it could indicate that perhaps this child is not on her way to becoming bilingual. Each one of these texts is a conversation starter, an opportunity for parents to learn more.

The text about the cat food, between a mom and her daughter, clearly shows that one cares about a school assignment and the other about the cat. Guess who cares more about the cat? On the surface, the text is chuckle-worthy. But it is also informative. This teenager obviously does not really want to discuss the "book thing," but then again, she opens the door for consideration. Writing is clearly not her favorite subject, but something about this possibility piqued her interest. She is willing to consider the idea. Sometimes the learning process needs to proceed slowly. This time, it happens by feeding the cat first, and then considering the "book thing."

The sweet, innocent text about the first crush is a testimonial to a trusting relationship between this parent and child. First crushes come with so many emotions, ups and downs, and possible heartbreaks. Perhaps this child was even more comfortable texting the information than sharing it in person.

Texts are not replacements for in-person interactions, but they can be embraced as opportunities to learn from and about your children using their language. Take the time to read between the lines. The messages are an avenue to build trust and acceptance. (Even if you learn your child cares more about the cat than school!)

SHARED ADVENTURES

The most important part of learning together is "together." Sometimes your child will be teaching you, sometimes the experience will be driven by your own interests, and sometimes the adventure will be equally new to both of you. Creating opportunities for your children to teach you is foundational for voice. This "flipping of the table" provides children an opportunity to shine, to share their knowledge and interests, and to be in the driver's seat. When an adventure is new to both of you, you learn to "drive" together.

Adventures don't have to be expensive or involve long-distance travel. For younger children, going to a park and learning a new recess-type game is an adventure. Older children may enjoy trying food from a new local food truck, shooting hoops, or showing you their latest skateboarding trick. Parents who have a long-distance relationship with their child can share online adventures, such as virtually touring a country, climbing a mountain, or coauthoring a blog.

One caution, no matter the age of your children: Be prepared that your child might not have the same enthusiastic experience that you do. You may love the learning and they may not. Have you

Photo courtesy of Russ Quaglia

ever taken your child to do something you thought would be super cool, only to discover she thought the adventure was lame? Did you go to a local farm only for your child to say, "I have seen a cow before"? What was your response? "Come on, this is fun!" "Give it a chance. You've never seen a cow up close like this before. How can you not like this? Next time, I will bring your sister."

It is disheartening when these efforts are met with a lackluster response, yet as parents we need to learn from this experience. Ask yourself:

- Did your child help plan the adventure?
- Was it too early in the morning? Too late in the day?
- Did she miss out on other plans to go with you?
- Was she really just not interested in that particular experience?

These reflections can shed light on planning for the next adventure. After all, the children should look forward to the experience. Most people learn better when they are enjoying the experience. A fun experience can go a long way in fostering relationships and laughter!

KEYS TO SINCERE LEARNING

Learning can occur after repeated failures, as well as from first-attempt successes. Learning might be an "ah ha" or "I finally get it!" moment. Learning might be demonstrated in a child taking his first step or a teenager learning to drive. Learning is all around us—some of it occurs with a conscious effort driven by interest (playing the guitar) or a need (fixing a broken bike), and some of it simply occurs naturally, without a second thought, through our daily experiences. That is also true of our learning with our children. Some learning is built in—inherent in the relationship and time spent together. But we should be more intentional than that; we should make a consistently conscious effort to connect and learn with our children in ways that engage them. This can be achieved in an atmosphere that fosters *Acceptance, Inquisitiveness, Openness,* and *Patience.*

Acceptance: Children need to know that their parents accept them for who they are. You may want your child to be athletic, but he prefers artistic endeavors. You may want your child to love fishing, but he can't bear the thought of hooking a fish. You may want your child to aspire to run the family shop, yet she is passionate about cooking. Ultimately, they are their own people. When children believe that their parents accept them for who they are, they can become more confident in themselves and in their relationship with you. With this acceptance comes a level of comfort in sharing and a willingness to learn together.

REFLECT—ACCEPTANCE

- *How do you let your child know that you want her to be her own person?*
- *In what ways do you show your child that you are proud of her?*

Inquisitiveness: Some learning occurs out of necessity. Many of us would happily forego needing to learn how to do our taxes, take a test, or negotiate rent. But learning out of curiosity is in a category by itself. This involves a desire to know more, to do more, or to try more—all for the sake of finding out. Think about the level of excitement connected to "mandatory learning," as compared to the excitement of learning because you *want* to know something. For some children, a great deal of their school experience feels like mandatory learning; classes are boring and subjects are uninspiring. While their curiosity may change from class to class or year to year, it is no fun feeling like learning is something to just get through. Offering your child opportunities to explore her own passions and curiosities with you fosters inquisitiveness. Try things that are outside both of your comfort zones. Are you afraid of the ocean? Visit an aquarium. Not a huge sports fan? Go cheer on the local team. Never painted before? Create a mural together. Hate to exercise? Try walking somewhere new. And if your child happens to love camping and you prefer a hotel room, well, you might just have to suffer through a few bug bites, unshowered days, and burnt meals around the fire pit to learn about his passion.

- *What was the last thing you and your child learned together?*
- *How do you create opportunities for your child to share his excitement with you?*

Openness: Being open requires a willingness to be vulnerable. Do your children know your political beliefs? Do they know your thoughts on changes within your own community, whether positive or negative? Do they know your hopes and aspirations for yourself and them? These insights allow you and your children to grow together, debate, disagree, and find common passions.

Openness involves parents sharing their successes, as well as their failures. Parents aren't always perfect, and it is okay for children to see our imperfections. For example, if you don't know how to work the remote, change a flat tire, or figure out how to use the latest cell phone app, then admit it! When children recognize their parents as individuals with their own levels of confidence and insecurities, they start to see their "human side." This fosters everyone's ability to be open about who they are, what they are interested in, what they believe in, and what they want to learn about.

REFLECT—OPENNESS

- *What failures have you experienced that you shared with your children?*
- *What was your last success that you shared with your children?*

Patience: "I have heard that story 1,000 times!" It is somehow ironic that young and old alike repeat stories. Who hasn't heard a parent or grandparent tell the same story more than once? Our children, similar to our parents, may tell us the same stories or jokes repeatedly and usually with the same enthusiasm as the first time. It is this latter point that matters. Our children get joy out of sharing the information or humor with others. As parents, we need to simply be patient and laugh one more time. A few classics heard dozens of times:

Q: Why was 6 afraid of 7?

A: Because 7, 8, 9

Knock, knock.
-Who's there?

Banana.
-Banana who?

Knock, knock.
-Who's there?

Banana.
-Banana who?

Knock, knock.
-Who's there?

Orange.
-Orange who?

Orange you glad I didn't say banana?

Q: What do you call an old snowman?

A: Water

Laugh again, and keep in mind that these stories are your child's way of sharing and engaging with you. The jokes will eventually change, and there will even come a day when you look back on them longingly. Meanwhile, embrace the repetition as your child's way of connecting and learning together.

 REFLECT—PATIENCE

- *What do you remember overtelling as a kid—a joke? A story? Facts?*

- *What strategies do you use when you feel your patience is running thin?*

Opportunities to learn from and with our children present themselves every day, in various ways. We can learn about our son's sense of humor when talking about everyday events. We can learn more (or at least refresh our memories!) about algebra in order to support him when he is struggling with that course. We can learn more ways to be empathetic when we see our son supporting a new student or standing up for a classmate who is being teased. The opportunities are endless; the key is to consistently remain aware and capture as many as we can. Capitalizing on the myriad learning opportunities will be different for each parent and child, driven by individual interests, personalities, family routines, and beliefs.

Mom's Musings on Learning

When I was a boy of fourteen, my father was so igno-rant I could hardly stand to have the old man around. But when I got to be twenty-one, I was astonished by how much he'd learned in seven years.

Mark Twain

All moms (and I am sure dads) come to realize at some point that they actually know nothing at all. Well, maybe we don't actually realize it, but our teenagers often try to convince us of it! All too quickly, we are in situations where we can no longer help with homework (did I really take calculus?), we are not familiar with the coolest artists and bands (when did Bruce Springsteen stop being cool?), we run a bit slower than we used to, and we can't understand the appeal of binge-watching a Netflix series. It can prove challenging to show your child you are willing to learn when he or she thinks you are beyond hope. Parents must be relentless in their commitment to learn from their children. Otherwise, we run the risk of becoming obsolete!

Photo courtesy of Kris Fox

My (KF) youngest daughter is a culinary student. She hails from a family of foodies. Her grandmother (Gram) loves to cook, her great-grandmother (nicknamed Pasta Fagioli) wouldn't even consider making anything from a box, and her father constantly looks forward to the next meal. My daughter's culinary competition as a freshman in high school required endless trials making crab cakes at home. At first, I was honored to be the taster. But then my advice started creeping in (after all, I had made crab cakes before!). After a few "helpful" tips, I caught myself. This undertaking was not about my advice or teaching; it was about my daughter showing me how to cook crab cakes. Guess what? I didn't know as much as I thought. I learned that it is tastier to use scallions than regular onions.

Far too many tastings later (thank goodness she wasn't making meatloaf), she perfected her recipe, I learned some new techniques, and she went on to compete. Although I cannot imagine ever eating another crab cake, it was rewarding to spend a week learning from my daughter.

Lesson Learned: Let your child be the expert. You'll be surprised by what you learn!

Dad's Deliberations on Learning

I (RQ) recently become a grandfather. Yes, it is amazing. And of course, my granddaughter is perfect. I had anticipated how special this feeling would be, but it has exceeded even that. At times, I am overwhelmed with emotion as I gaze into Adlee's eyes and see a world of wonder. Other times, I watch as my daughter Lauren (Lo) and her husband Arik interact with Adlee and see incredible happiness and pride. It is moments like these that we can take comfort in the fact that we did something right. We developed the foundation for our daughter to become the best parent she can possibly be. One would naturally think it would be a time for Papi (me) to impart more knowledge and wisdom to my daughter. After all, there are so many things that I wanted to instinctively share:

Photo courtesy of Russ Quaglia

Be careful of the baby's head.

It is fine to let her cry.

Make sure you burp her.

Be careful of the dog near the baby.

But then I realized it wasn't my turn. And Lo didn't need to learn anything from me. It was time for Papi to learn from the interactions of my daughter with her daughter. So instead of imparting knowledge, I asked questions and learned about parenting in today's world. I asked what websites she uses for new moms, how we can see Adlee over Skype, how mommy meet-ups work, and how the heck Amazon Prime delivers diapers in two hours! My granddaughter has provided another opportunity for me to learn from my own kids.

I observed how patient my daughter is with Adlee, even when her crying seems relentless. I witnessed something that I have been telling my children for years "Having the right attitude is way more important than doing something right." Lo was resolute and disciplined to never become discouraged when things were going sideways. Instead, she became more determined to learn and find a solution. From the start, Lo handled things like she has been a mother for 20 years, not 20 days! I could not be more proud.

In those moments, I saw the past and the future simultaneously. It was a meaningful reminder that what we do as parents impacts how our children will interact with their own children. I feel more fortunate than ever seeing my daughter love and adore my granddaughter in the same way I love and adore her.

As a side note, I can tell you Lo and Arik are far more knowledgeable about raising a child than I was! They have more books on raising children than I ever knew existed. I can only hope this book finds its way on to their bookshelf!

Lesson Learned: Even when we have worthwhile experiences and wisdom to share, it is important to let our children be the leaders and learn even more.

REFLECT ON LEARNING

- *What are some of the things your child has taught you?*
- *What frustrates you the most when learning with your child? Why?*
- *What are you excited to learn about from your child?*

LEARNING: TAKE ACTION

Throughout life, the child is more often in the position of learning from the parent than vice versa. It is important to acknowledge that there is a great deal that parents can learn from their children and to remain open to that learning on a regular basis. Start by getting their feedback. Ask your child to rate you on the following items, responding with **Always**, **Sometimes**, or **Never**.

1. I know and respect your current interests.

2. I create time to learn from you.

3. I am patient with you.

4. I share my own opinions and ideas with you.

5. I am willing to try new things with you.

Keep in mind that how your child rates you is somewhat fluid. It may be influenced by a recent interaction and reflective of how he is feeling in response to that situation. While it may not always

PARENT VOICE

reflect how he would "score" you overall, it is a valid measure of how he is feeling at that time and a great springboard for discussion and action. The following are some strategies for learning with your children.

INSTEAD OF KNOWING IT ALL, TRY REALIZING NO ONE DOES!

With longevity (a.k.a. age) comes lots of experiences, wisdom, and knowledge. Be wary, however, of developing the "been there, done that" frame of mind that can lead to "inside the box" thinking. Adults are less inclined to "see" that the sky does not have to be colored blue or that dessert can come before dinner. Maybe the way things have always been done is not the correct way, only way, or best way. To learn from a child, adults must be willing to forgo what they think they know and accept the wisdom, insights, and wonders of youth.

INSTEAD OF DOING IT QUICKLY YOURSELF, TRY SLOWING DOWN AND WORKING TOGETHER

Have you ever started cooking a meal with your child, only to find yourself measuring most of the ingredients? Have you ever tried to help your child with an assignment only to realize you did most of the work? Have you ever picked out your kindergartner's outfits despite promising to let her dress herself before school? It can be easier to complete a project yourself, rather than letting your child do parts independently. However, these actions eliminate the learning and the "shared" part of the experience. It can take more time to achieve the goal, and it may require more patience, but it is certainly worth the time to allow your child to learn. And it can be more fun!

INSTEAD OF COMPLETING THOUGHTS, TRY SUPPORTING INDEPENDENT THINKING

Think about the infamous school science fair projects. Every year, countless middle school students develop poster boards explaining one of about fifteen different experiments. If you have experienced this, you are already aware of most of the results. Plants will die in the dark, certain mediums conduct electricity, and mold grows on bread. While it can be tempting to correct your child's conclusions when you already know the results, it is important to keep in mind that this experience is new to your child. Let him analyze the results and draw his own conclusions, even if they are wrong. A great deal of learning comes from mistakes and incorrect conclusions.

INSTEAD OF ACCEPTING THE STATUS QUO, TRY MOVING OUTSIDE YOUR COMFORT ZONE

Sometimes we fall into routines without even realizing it—rotating through certain meals for dinner or mindlessly watching the same TV shows or replaying the same disagreements or debates. Challenge yourself and your children to rethink your routines. While participating in activities that stretch your comfort level can produce anxiety, they can also result in the most rewarding learning. Never ridden a dirt bike? Hit the trails. Never eaten Indian food or fish? Surprise your taste buds. Never watched a foreign movie? Get ready for subtitles. Never ventured outside your neighborhood? Try visiting a new area. Apply this type of thinking to other categories that have become routine.

INSTEAD OF WORRYING ABOUT PERFECTION, TRY *FOCUSING ON PROGRESS*

Have you ever proofed your child's writing homework and wondered how he passed last year's English class? Or, have you witnessed your child play a sport only to wonder if she understood *any* of the rules? It can be so easy to go through the homework with him and help him correct every single capitalization and punctuation mistake to make the perfect "A" paper. But then what happens on the next assignment . . . and the one after that, and the one after that? It is more effective to help your child understand the appropriate use of capitals and commas, and apply them correctly in a few instances in the paper. This leads to learning and progress. Likewise, a child's shortcomings on the athletic field don't mean she should quit. She may just not be a superstar, and that is okay. If she is enjoying it and progressing as a player, then that is a valuable experience. A parent's desire for getting it exactly right all the time or being the best can sometimes cloud the celebration of progress.

INSTEAD OF JUMPING TO THE NEXT TASK, TRY *REFLECTING*

In this age of technology, our lives are more fast paced than ever. Everybody needs everything done yesterday. Learning, however, should be a reflective process. It should include time to reflect on content, options, and actions. Take the time to reflect on choices that were made and decide if they were the best decisions or if something could have been done differently to create a better outcome. Be willing to share reflections on your choices, as well as help your child reflect on his own decisions. Talk with your child about whether he is learning or memorizing information, blindly following directions or comprehending assignments, or rushing through projects simply to start watching the latest viral video.

When it comes to learning with our children, there can always be obstacles, be it scheduling logistics, interest levels, or energy levels. While it would be convenient if there was a single guaranteed approach for success, this is more of a give-it-a-try-and-see-what-happens effort. Be consistent and sincere in your invitations to your children to teach you and learn with you. Offer a range of suggestions—those that readily align with their interests and those that are outside everyone's comfort zone. Some of them are bound to hit the mark!

Learning Through the Years

This section presents ideas to help parents better understand and practice learning with children of various ages. As with all developmental recommendations, keep in mind that not all children fit neatly into their age category. Consider which descriptors best suit your child and follow the recommendations for that age range.

4- to 7-Year-Olds

Learn to Explain Themselves

- Ask specific questions that help guide your child in gathering her thoughts.
- Be patient, allowing your child to find his words instead of finishing his sentences for him.

Emerge as Readers

- Ask your child what he thinks the story is about, using clues from the pictures.

- Be cognizant of the reading level of projects you do. Directions that are too challenging will discourage children from learning with you.

Look for Guidance

- Refrain from immediately providing advice. Some children find it easier to simply be told what to do rather than have to learn a new skill.

- Ask for your child's opinion on issues where her voice matters.

Learn From Siblings and Peers

- Encourage your children to take turns learning from each other.

- Talk with your child about what she has learned from peers.

8- to 10-Year Olds

Spend Significant Time on Electronics

- Create a device-free time every day when parents and children put their devices in a central location and tune into each other.

- If you can't beat them, join them. Consider downloading interactive apps where you and your child play games, learn a new skill, or compete through the app.

(Continued)

(Continued)

Experience Self-consciousness

- Help children understand that everyone has different learning styles. Celebrate the ways your child learns.

- Acknowledge that everyone has insecurities. With your child, discuss his and your own.

Share Ideas With Hesitation

- Provide your child with choices of specific things she can share. "Tell me about the game you played in P.E. or a joke you heard today."

- Share something with your child that you learned each day.

Tune Out Others' Ideas and Suggestions

- Work with your child on taking turns when it comes to sharing ideas. For every idea he shares, have him ask a sibling or parent to share an idea.

- Be sure collaborative learning involves the children and is not adult-directed.

11- to 13-Year-Olds

Desire Independence

- Let your children know that good decision making involves using resources, including their parents!

- Discuss current events and moral issues. Help your children see both sides of issues and talk about ways to make informed personal decisions.

Remain in Comfort Zone

- Encourage your child to try new things and broaden his horizons.
- Share your interests and invite your child to join you.

Spend Time With Peers Instead of Parents

- Continue to offer to drive groups of kids to their various activities, and encourage your child to invite friends over. These are ways to see firsthand what their interests are.
- Ask questions! It is important to ask your child what he enjoys, who his close friends are, and what they enjoy doing in their free time.

Overlook Connection Between Present Learning and Future Benefits

- Help your child establish a goal one week or month away and make a specific plan together for how to achieve that.
- Discuss life after high school. And then discuss this again and again!

14- to 18-Year-Olds

Seek Separation From Parents

- Expect some conflict. This is a natural part of your teenager becoming independent.
- Respect your teenager's opinions, even when they differ from your own. Listen and learn from your teen's point of view.

(Continued)

(Continued)

Think About the Future

- Know your teenager's hopes and dreams. Support them in the efforts to take steps today that will help them achieve their dreams for tomorrow.

- Learn about world events together. Talk with your teenager about what is important to him and how he would like to make a difference in the world.

Stress About School

- Talk with your teenager about what is easy and what is challenging for her at school. Celebrate her efforts and provide support for what she finds challenging.

- Discuss with your teenager and his teacher his schedule to confirm he is placed appropriately in classes, considering requirements, work load, and interests.

Struggle With Motivation

- Model motivation and excitement. It can be contagious.

- Work with your teenager to find opportunities that allow her to grow and explore interests.

OUR LEARNING FROM PARENTS AND CHILDREN

We love our professional opportunities to speak with parents and students. Their experiences are as varied as the students we meet. Some parents juggle the personalities and schedules of multiple children, while others wonder about how to make sure their only child connects with other children at school. Some parents share their own anxieties about becoming involved with their child's school, whether from their own experiences as students or because English is not their primary language. Some parents share stories about how their children coordinate and communicate their school experiences between two households, and others talk about the challenges of being a foster care parent.

We always appreciate what parents share with us, and we always learn something new. More often than not, we learn something that makes us smile as well. We often ask parents and children the exact same question, yet receive very different responses. Some of the sentiments we commonly hear around learning are shown below.

CHILDREN SAY . . .	PARENTS SAY . . .
My parents don't understand me.	*My kids forget that I was a kid once, too.*
I hate math.	*My daughter wants to be an engineer.*
My parents' interests aren't mine.	*How can my kid not like . . .?*
My parents ask too many questions.	*My kid never answers me.*
I just cleaned my room.	*How can my kid find anything in that mess?*
I don't want to go to college.	*My kid can't wait to go to college.*
My parents want me to be perfect.	*I just want my kid to be happy.*
I just want my parents to understand me.	*I just want my children to know I care.*
My parents hate my boyfriend.	*My teenager doesn't have a boyfriend.*

Think about how you and your children perceive, experience, or respond to the same moments very differently. Learning often requires clarification. Parents should keep in mind that children show excitement and enthusiasm in different ways. "Even though I wasn't all smiles and giggles, I really did have fun!" A child may not appear wildly excited on the outside or may even display the quintessential teenage sullenness, but that doesn't mean they don't appreciate learning together!

NEVER STOP LEARNING

We learn things from the day we are born, and most of it seems to be from people older than ourselves: our parents, teachers, neighbors, friends of parents, aunts, uncles, grandparents, and older kids in school. We are asking you to be willing to learn from someone younger, from your own children. As parents, we legitimately know a great deal, but even we have to admit that we do not know everything. And even when we think we know best, we sometimes miss the mark. It is natural to fall back on what we know and how we were brought up, and teach our children accordingly. But times have changed, faster than any of us could have imagined:

Remember when the phone in your kitchen was connected to the wall, and there was such a thing as a phone book? Now virtually every kid over the age of eight has his own cell phone with a scrolling list of phone numbers.

Remember when the most innovative video games consisted of a rectangular paddle (that only moved vertically) and a ball? Now the players can interact with the characters in the video games.

Remember when you actually had to go to the library to look up information? Now every kid has instantaneous access to world news and events at the tips of their thumbs.

Remember when you had to drive to the store to rent a video? Now movies are delivered to your mailbox or streamed to your mobile device.

Remember when Amazon Prime didn't exist and you actually had to go to the store to buy something?

Remember when all cars ran on gasoline?

Yes, times have certainly changed. But has the way we parent kept up? Of course, some aspects of parenting remain constant through generations, as they should: unconditional love, hope for a happy and healthy future, and being there when our children need us, even when they don't realize they do. Those things will never wane. But if we are going to give the best of ourselves to our kids and provide them with the guidance they need to be the best *they* can be, we must be ready and willing to learn from them. We must be prepared to learn about the world *they* are growing up in and to learn how we can best support them in achieving *their* aspirations. Our past is not our children's future. It is okay to be nervous about this, but it is important to embrace the idea that our children have something to teach us.

CHAPTER 4

Lead

Working in Harmony
With Your Child and School

No one can whistle a symphony. It takes a whole orchestra to play it.

—H.E. Luccock

When my (RQ) children were younger, I worked in various school districts where I engaged in meaningful, shared leadership with my colleagues all the time. As someone who advocates for student voice, the irony occurred to me. I rarely considered shared leadership with my own children. In an effort to change, I embarked on my ... I mean *our* ... first leadership venture. On the way home from their after-school rec programs one evening, we stopped for dinner at one of their favorite places, Governor's in Orono, Maine. My kids were nine, seven, and six at the time.

Up until that point, I had the habit of telling my kids what they could eat at restaurants and, in many instances, ordering for them. But that was all about to change. They were going to have ownership of their meal for the first time! I proudly announced, "Tonight, you can order anything you want, and I will not say a word!" For further emphasis, I told the kids what I wanted, asked them to order for me, and left the table. They were given responsibility for making their own decisions. Once the server took their order, I returned and did not even ask what they had selected. I wanted to be pleasantly surprised. After about 10 minutes, I saw my cheeseburger with fries heading our way. On the same tray, I saw three ice cream sundaes and a piece of apple pie.

While I was working through my not-as-pleasant-as-I-thought feeling of surprise, my oldest daughter, Lauren, proudly said, "Dad, we wanted to surprise you and get you a piece of pie to go with your burger!" All I could focus on was how the heck they decided to order ice cream for dinner instead of the usual grilled cheese sandwich or a hot dog, and there they were, all beaming because they did something so thoughtful for me! My takeaways from this shared leadership experience were:

1. My parenting skills were nonexistent when it came to nutrition.

2. My *wanting* my kids to make good decisions was distinct from them *actually making* good decisions.

3. Giving kids choices is fine. Giving them choices without parameters is foolish.

4. My kids were right . . . apple pie does make me happy!

With practice and a bit more guidance, my children eventually learned how to order responsibly, and their investment in independent food choices carried over into their school lunch choices, which had previously been packed by yours truly.

LEADING MATTERS

Parents want their children to be leaders, and teachers want their students to model leadership—not necessarily as the class president or team captain but as leaders in their own right. They want students to make sound decisions, stand up for what they believe in, and consider others before they act. Children do not need a formal position or a title to be leaders, and they do not need to wait around for an invitation to lead. Contrary to popular thinking, leading is anything but a solo endeavor. Great leaders develop relationships, and there are no winners or losers. If my idea "wins" over your idea, then it is not a successful relationship. If my idea and your idea become *our* idea, then we have success. The real victory is in developing a shared understanding and an ability to work together. Children need genuine opportunities to make decisions, and they need support throughout the process—both when they succeed and when they fail.

Ensuring children have opportunities to make responsible decisions requires a willingness from parents to lead *with* their children, rather than *for* their children. Leading *with* children means allowing them to be part of the decision-making process, including understanding the consequences, positive and/or negative, of decisions. Leading *for* children means a parent makes decisions that impact the child with no involvement or input from that child. The former requires more time, effort, and patience, but it is an authentic way for children to learn how to make responsible decisions, both at school and in life. For example, consider an older sibling who picks up and cares for her younger sibling after school. A parent could provide all the instructions in a To Do and Not To Do list of instructions. While this may be efficient, the older sibling is charged with a significant responsibility, yet is given no opportunity for ownership in the learning and leading of the situation. A more effective approach for involving the older sibling would be to discuss the challenges and responsibilities that come with watching a sibling, discuss how to address them, and develop a contingency plan. Not only will the older child learn more but she will be more apt to be engaged and invested in the task for which she is left responsible.

Children often experience people (parents, teachers, employers) in leadership positions as having power or control over them. In fact, parents may experience schools as having control over the educational choices for their children. And schools experience parents as having control over final decisions, even though they may not have the educational expertise. *Power over* is prevalent all around us. However, leadership that relies solely on power promotes compliance and blind obedience, whereas leadership that shares decision making promotes commitment and responsibility.

Parents and schools have a common goal: helping children become thoughtful, considerate, independent thinkers who accept the responsibility that accompanies the decisions they make throughout their lives. As parents define their role within the home-school relationship, they will find there are many fine lines, including those between:

- being an involved parent . . . and being an overbearing parent
- helping a child with an assignment . . . and doing homework for her
- being proud of hard work . . . and only praising high grades
- trusting your child . . . and monitoring every decision he makes

Like so much in life, this is all about finding the right balance. How involved should you be to effectively support your child in school but not be overly controlling? For example, it is important to support your child's involvement in co-curricular activities but not dictate which activities he should do. How much do you trust your child to be independent, yet monitor his actions to be sure he is ok? Consider social media, for example. You want to trust your child to use online access responsibly, including for school assignments, but have a responsibility to make sure he is safe and accessing appropriate sites. There are no one-size-fits-all answers regarding how to balance respect and safety, but shared leadership can help determine what is most suitable for you and your child.

DIGGING DEEPER

Whether at home or school, it is crucial to listen to the voice of all children/students in order to lead together. No one should be left out. This notion is often expressed by the middle child, as she feels her voice is either drowned out by the older sibling who knows better or overshadowed by the younger sibling who always seems to get her way. A parent cannot assume that the voice of the older and younger sibling average out to represent the voice of the middle child. Similarly, in schools, a commitment must be made to listen to the voice of all students in order to make informed, meaningful decisions. Our work in schools is a constant reminder of this, as principals and teachers share the challenges they face in collecting the perspectives of all students. They must remember that not everyone in a subgroup has the same experiences or perspectives. Schools must dig deeper. Just because a student grows up in a certain neighborhood does not mean he will think the same way as every other child in that neighborhood. We must provide each student a forum for his voice if we are to lead together successfully. Accordingly, school leaders cannot rely on the voice of a few to represent the whole or any demographically defined subgroup (gender, race, ethnicity, SES, etc.). Meaningful relationships, and a commitment to creating a shared goal, have an underlying agreement that everyone involved has a voice in decision making.

DEVELOPING PARTNERSHIPS

Leading together cannot happen without a genuine partnership. Regardless of the age of your children, there are many opportunities when parents, children, and teachers can lead together in a manner that is informed by everyone's voice. The importance of partnership extends into one of the most constant balancing acts connected with school: homework. Whether you agree or disagree with the practice, students of all ages have homework. For many parents, students, and teachers, homework is dreaded.

Most students dread having to do hours of homework after a long day of school. Parents fear the evening battle, which can run the gamut of becoming over-involved to the "This is your homework. I already completed sixth grade!" approach. On the flip side, teachers despise seeing projects that appear to have been completed by professional artists and engineers, or hearing the infamous "My dog ate my homework" excuses. The solution is a partnership.

Several decades ago when we were in school, it was common for parents to have a more hands-off approach with school. Our parents did not keep tabs on what assignments were due and when. For one of us, that worked fine (KF). Grades were important to Dr. Fox, and she was self-driven to complete assignments. While a "good job" now and then would have been welcomed, no assignment was ever missed. (She was too nervous about getting in trouble or disappointing the teachers!) For another author (RQ), the parental hands-off approach may not have been the best match. Homework did not hold much meaning for Dr. Q—assignments were boring and they just did not seem to matter (at least not as much as sports and possibly getting into a little trouble). In both cases, support for homework and consequences for missed assignments were left entirely up to the school—the experts—to deal with or not. There was no balance between parent–student–school.

To develop a genuine partnership around homework, first ask yourself if you understand the school and your child's perspectives:

- What are the school's policies related to homework?
- Do you know what major assignments your child has due and when?
- Which assignments may cause anxiety for your child, and which will engage him?

Then think about your own perspective and knowledge of your family:

- Do you have a fear of math and, accordingly, believe there is no way you will be able to help your child with a math problem?
- Is there a regular weekday night when your child will have limited time to do homework due to other commitments?

Being informed of all perspectives is an important part of the parent-student-school relationship. Take, for example, a student who regularly misses assignments due on Friday. The easy default thinking is that the student simply does not take enough responsibility for his work. But it is often much more complicated than that. The parent, student, and teacher each have their own perspectives and realities.

The student may have a job on weekday evenings, could be in charge of younger siblings after school, may not understand an assignment, or simply does not like the class and chooses not to do the assignment.

The teacher may believe timely completion of assignments is important for continued learning, could foresee no excuse for incomplete assignments since they are given several days in advance and class time is provided, or may presume the student is lazy.

The parent may have no idea her child is missing assignments, may not understand the particular content enough to help, may work every evening, or may feel that homework is not her responsibility.

Successful partnerships begin with an understanding that almost all issues involve multiple perspectives and experiences that must be understood so fewer assumptions are made and more solutions are found. The teacher might have to be more flexible, the student might need to plan better and ask for help, and the parent might need to seek additional support for her student from the school or an outside tutor. Everyone involved in the partnership has some level of responsibility. The partnership approach where the parent, student, and school work together reduces anxiety for everyone involved (and decreases the chance of needing a "My dog ate my homework" excuse!).

SHARED GOALS

In order for a relationship between parent, child, and school to be effective, you must set the stage and have a shared goal in sight. Leading without established goals is aimless wandering. Leading without a clear understanding of who has a voice is misleading. Both can result in frustration and distrust in the relationship. Working together to understand the voice of everyone involved requires more patience but ultimately is worth the time and effort. When children are involved in the decision-making journey, they learn how to collaborate, compromise, take action, and assume responsibility.

For example, how many times do you have to ask your kids to get up in the morning? We averaged three requests per kid per morning. "Time to get up" turns into "Let's go. You are going to be late!" Followed by the final assertion, "This is the last time I am telling you to get up. If you're late, you're late!" After being the human snooze alarm for years, I (RQ) got to thinking . . . why *would* they get out of bed the first time when they know Dad will wake them up two more times? It was time for a family meeting. I asked my kids why it took three attempts to get them out of bed. The response from my oldest, Lauren, was pragmatic, "Well, you always get us up eventually." My son, Casey, noted that his alarm clock broke two years ago, and my youngest at the time, Chelsea, shrugged and said, "I don't know." Obviously, my kids were fine with me being inconvenienced each morning. It was time to get to the bottom of this.

I asked my kids if it was important to them to be on time for school. It was unanimous—yes! It appeared my goal, their goal, and I'm certain their teachers' goals, all aligned—be on time for school. So why was I the only one frustrated in the morning? Why did I have to work so hard to get them out of bed? Once my kids elaborated, it became clear: They wanted to be on time but still sleep as late as possible each day. That is where we differed. My goal was to have them wake up with time to eat breakfast, put on clean clothes without rushing around searching for them, brush their teeth, and be on time for school. Their goal was to get out of bed as late as possible and be on time for school, with breakfast and brushing optional and rushing accepted. They just wanted to be on time to avoid getting in trouble or receiving detention, which would interfere with their after-school activities.

While the motivations were different for my children and me, the core goal of timeliness was shared. It was the related details that needed to be worked out. With each person having a chance to voice their opinions and ideas, we devised a plan. The kids agreed that they should indeed have some food before school and clean their teeth after they eat it. I agreed to prepare the breakfast. How fast they got dressed and how much they had to run around doing it was up to them. Each child got a new alarm clock, and, given his propensity for snoozing, Casey asked his sister to wake him up if he hit the snooze button too many times. We all agreed that they were old enough to assume some responsibility for achieving the shared goal (and Dad's morning time would be better spent with a cup of coffee!).

With the plan firmly established, I stopped waking them up. My snooze functionality ceased to exist. WOW. . .what a morning that first morning was! Lauren and Casey missed their bus. They walked to school with breakfast in hand. They got detentions for being late, and poor Chelsea missed a test first period. While it was a tough lesson, rest assured (pun intended), they all got up on their own, and on time, from that day forward!

KEYS TO LEADING SUCCESSFULLY

Leading is a lifelong skill, one that is valuable in school, on teams, in jobs, and in relationships. It involves working together to brainstorm ideas, solve problems, and take action. As you work with your child to develop a productive parent-student-school partnership for leading, foster the following key attributes: *prioritize, teamwork, decision making,* and *responsibility.*

Prioritize: Parenting is a juggling act, albeit not always entertaining! Every parent has times when they are busy, stressed, overwhelmed—times when the calendar somehow has more than 24 hours' worth of commitments scheduled into a single day. Time is every parent's nemesis. It is unrealistic to think any parent can lead with their children on all decisions. Decisions that are solely the parent's aside, the remaining opportunities for shared leadership must be prioritized. Be selective. When you consider how and when to get involved in school issues, first think about which issues and concerns matter most to you and your children. You may not be concerned that a particular co-curricular activity is being dropped. Yet, it may matter significantly that the school district is considering changing free and reduced breakfast plans or switching school uniforms to a more expensive version. You and your child can decide to which issues you lend your voice.

It is also important to consider which issues you can truly impact. In an ideal, timeless world, parents, students, and teachers would discuss all important school issues together. Schools would hold focus groups with children and parents to understand their perspectives before making decisions. But there simply is not enough time. Some decisions need to be made by the school in conjunction with district considerations, such as the start time and scheduling teacher in-service days. Other decisions can be immediately impacted by the input from students and parents, such as any safety concerns at the school. Prioritize your and your child's interests and then get involved with issues where your voice can make a difference.

REFLECT—PRIORITIZE

- *How do you prioritize what matters most to you and your children at school?*

- *How do you allow your child to prioritize his life related to school, sports, and work?*

Photo courtesy of Deb Young

Teamwork: Teamwork is the backbone of shared leadership; without it, everything falls apart. Teamwork includes parents, children, and teachers working together to solve a problem or create a new idea. Perhaps one of the best examples of teamwork involves something referred to as the "walking school bus." We work in several locations where elementary students walk to school, yet they walk through unsafe neighborhoods. This is an issue for everyone—children and parents feel safety concerns, and the school often notices students are frequently absent. Although the "walking school bus" probably looks different in different communities, the basic idea is that a parent walks groups of students to school. We have seen dads, in particular, work together to take walking shifts. They start at one designated spot in their neighborhood and walk to school, "picking up" kids along the way. By the time the dads reach the school, there is a "busload" of kids arriving safely. Now that's teamwork!

REFLECT—TEAMWORK

- *How do you take a team approach to solving school problems?*
- *When have you experienced teamwork at your child's school?*

Decision Making: Decisions are made all the time every day, by parents, children, and teachers. It is impossible to lead without making decisions. Yet, decision making is not necessarily intuitive. Someone who is never provided opportunities to make decisions may find himself at a loss when considering options and choices. Recall the first time you were faced with a new decision—how to spend money you had earned yourself, how to handle being fired from a job, how to handle a playground disagreement, etc. At every age, there are always new decisions to be made.

Children who have experience making decisions gain valuable insights with the process itself and are well prepared to make decisions throughout their lives.

In addition to the independent decisions, there are situations that require collaborative decision making. This is a life skill that will apply in school, careers, and relationships. There is no better place to start practicing joint decision making than at home and school. As parents, we can support our children by providing genuine opportunities to share their voice in discussions with their peers, teachers, and coaches, and to participate in the decision-making process.

 ## REFLECT—DECISION MAKING

- *What opportunities do you provide your children to be independent decision makers?*
- *In what ways do you collaborate with your children when making decisions that affect them?*

Responsibility: Leading requires a sense of responsibility to ourselves and others. Virtually all children want more autonomy and leadership opportunities, but they must be ready to handle the responsibility, and parents must be willing to provide opportunities for their children to take on responsibility. Eventually, our children will be responsible for themselves—their decisions, actions, and consequences. Children must decide, "Can I live with this decision?" "Is this a good decision for me?" Responsibility toward others involves understanding how one's actions and decisions impact other people. Both positive and negative decisions have consequences. Deciding to get involved in a fight at school affects your child and those around him negatively. Whereas, deciding to stand up to bullies has positive consequences for your child and the students he supports. Making responsible choices is a sign that your child is ready to lead with you and others.

REFLECT—RESPONSIBILITY

- *How do you help your children consider the consequences of their actions?*
- *What responsibilities do you find challenging to share with your children?*

PROACTIVE VOICE AT SCHOOL

Parent voice at school can face many of the same struggles as parent voice at home. Parent voice can be heard as noise, succumb to "selective hearing," or garner the adult equivalent of the eye roll. Many parents face personal hurdles to fostering their voice in schools, such as work commitments during the day, lack of transportation, and insufficient knowledge about the most current educational practices. Just as each parent-child relationship is unique, so is each parent-student-school relationship, with each person approaching it from her own unique perspective.

Parents share with us that while they are invited to be part of school committees, the focus is often dispensing information rather than inviting parent perspectives. These experiences do not reflect an inclusion of parent voice and meaningful involvement but rather parent representation. At the same time, principals and teachers report that parents are often quick to judge and react rather than listen and truly learn about the school's perspective. While schools and parents have a shared goal—creating the best learning environment for the students—these dueling experiences can create a challenging climate for parent and student voice at school. In addition, some parents prefer not to be involved and truly believe that school should be left to the experts—the teachers. Teachers are certainly experts in teaching, yet *you* are the expert on your children. A relationship mentality ("we") is much more productive than a divisive attitude ("us" versus "them"). Teachers need your input, ideas, and support. A positive parent-teacher relationship leads to a better teaching and learning environment for students.

Consider the difference a parent-student-teacher partnership makes in school conferences. Traditionally, schools hold parent-teacher conferences to update parents on their child's progress. This was historically the norm, and parents and educators did not really question the approach. However, this incomplete partnership was missing the most important person—the student. It is like taking your child to the doctor's office for a checkup without actually bringing her along. Have you ever been in a situation where someone talks for you and, even though well intended, conveys the wrong message? Students should be active participants in conferences, sharing their experiences at school, insights about their learning, and thoughts about meaningful goals.

We have participated in parent-teacher conferences where it seemed that both parties were talking about different children:

Teacher: "He is so organized and prompt with handing in his assignments."

Parent:	"He does his homework at the last minute every night and is always running late for school and practices!"
Teacher:	"He was really engaged throughout our marine biology unit."
Parent:	"I think he hates school as he never talks about it."

Either the parent and teacher are really talking about two different students, or they need to learn from the student. When parents, students, and teachers work together and share feedback, everyone works more effectively to support the student's learning. Involving students this way increases their sense of ownership in the process. Any information that is shared and decisions that are made at a conference have a direct impact on the student.

Even with the best intentions on the part of both school and home, relationships can be challenging. Respecting all perspectives and using a proactive voice will help make it more productive. As a parent, make a positive difference by decreasing parent noise and increasing parent voice at school.

PARENT NOISE	PARENT VOICE
Complain	Ask questions and understand; resist jumping to criticism.
Prejudge	Ask yourself what firsthand knowledge you have of a situation and be open to understanding both sides of an issue.
Show up	Be engaged and take action: Ask questions, listen to others, collaborate, offer solutions, and assist with implementation.
Email overload	Seek one-on-one, in-person conversations for important issues.
Gossip	Choose to make your voice a positive influence in the community.

Mom's Musings on Leading

At my (KF) daughter's school, teachers post grades and homework assignments online. This approach can be great, as students and parents have access to assignments. For one particular class, however, this did not fare so well. Over her week-long Thanksgiving break, my daughter thought she had an assignment to complete for this class. She regularly checked on the portal and with her friends. No assignments were posted. Although she was clearly stressed, I assured my daughter that since nothing was on the portal (I double checked myself), there must not be any assignment due.

On her first day back to school, my daughter texted me just before the start of the school day and said, "Crap! There is an assignment due today." I checked the portal and texted back, "No assignment posted." The next text from my daughter read, "LOOK NOW." Sure enough, the assignment was posted. My daughter called during lunch and asked if I could pick her up early. The assignment was due last period, and if she was absent from the class, she would be able to turn it in the next day without a penalty.

This was a significant dilemma for me (as a parent and an educator). On one hand, I really felt it was unfair to the students that the assignment was not posted prior to the break. On the other hand, I felt my daughter and her teacher should figure this out, and I should not intervene at this point. If the entire class did not do the assignment, surely there was no way they would all receive zeros. This was a life lesson, of sorts. I decided not to pick her up. Hindsight being 20/20, I think I was wrong. My daughter did attend class that day, and the teacher refused to accept late assignments. She received a zero for the assignment, even though she had attended every class, had never missed an assignment, and this assignment was not posted until the morning it was due. The assignment was weighted as much as a test and brought her grade for the semester down an entire letter grade.

My daughter had acted responsibly. Nothing lazy or lackadaisical about this; she wanted to complete the assignment. What further responsibility did I think I was giving her by making her stick it out? A lesson that life isn't fair? A lesson that the teacher is always right? A lesson that grades do not matter? Had I really been listening, learning, and leading with my child, I would have picked her up. I would have supported her decision based on what she knew the consequences would be rather than decide *for* her that the responsible thing to do was attend class. I also would have made an appointment with the teacher and my child to understand this dilemma and work collaboratively toward a solution for the future.

Lesson Learned: Parents do not always know best. We need to be prepared to listen more closely, learn from our children, and collaborate, particularly when they are the ones involved in the dilemma and will be the recipients of the consequences.

Dad's Deliberations on Leading

Throughout this book, we have addressed relationships between parents and their children, parents and their child's teacher, and all three working together. One relationship that has not been addressed is between parent, child, and coach. There are many coaches in schools, from the chess club to the drama club to various sports. My (RQ) coaching experience comes from the athletic side of things. I was a high school hockey coach for several years. Interestingly, it was in a town where the university team won the National Championship twice. Even more interesting, every parent in that community thought his child was ready to be drafted by the NHL and play in the All-Star game.

I coached because I loved the sport and the relationships I developed with the players. It was all about the team. What I did not enjoy was dealing with parents. My genius approach during my first month of coaching was to ignore the parents. I was annoyed by their behavior. They yelled at their kids from the stands during a game, screamed at the refs, and of course did not hold back from telling me how I should coach differently. From telling me their kid should play more to advising me to be more aggressive on the bench (a.k.a. yell at the players), every parent had a voice.

Recognizing that my brilliant ignoring approach was not having the effect I wanted and that I had already gone way past my tolerance level, I decided to have a team meeting, with the parents. Yes, a meeting with everyone—players, coaches, and parents. I asked my players what they liked about playing on the team. They all said they loved hockey because it was fun and full of action. And, of course, they enjoyed winning. I then asked them what they didn't like about playing. Most common reply? "My parents!" The parents were shocked. I was not. When I asked the parents the same two questions, they had many answers for the first question but none for the second. Not one parent complained about me, other players, the officiating, or anything else. It was fascinating to witness how parent voice can change so dramatically when parents are held accountable for what they say.

Sometimes the best way forward is only seen in hindsight. I should have had this meeting right at the start of the season. It showed me that even though everyone wanted to win (some more than others), only when I took the time to build relationships with parents would we be complete as a team. That meeting was a turning point. There was no more yelling from the stands, and we went on to have a great season (despite one win that got away . . . we lost in the state finals).

Lesson Learned: To this day, I still see overzealous parents in the stands yelling obnoxiously at kids and coaches. I know that will never change until the coaches, players, and parents come together and share their thoughts. To all those parents who continue to yell at the kids from the stands, I have two words for you. . . Stuff it! There are so many more productive ways to use your voice.

REFLECT ON LEADING

- *What have you learned from your child that changed the way you lead?*

- *How can you teach your child to be a responsible decision maker?*

- *In what ways do you foster a home-school relationship?*

LEADING: TAKE ACTION

Leading *with* our children is a more involved process than leading *for* them. They learn that their voice matters, that they are capable of making decisions, and that they are responsible for the related consequences. Leading *with* our children is an approach that ultimately serves them better. Start by getting their feedback. Ask your child to rate you on the following items, responding with **Always, Sometimes,** or **Never.**

1. We discuss and establish your goals for school together.

2. I involve you in decisions that impact you at school.

3. I ask you what matters most to you at school.

4. I support you when you succeed *and* when you fail.

5. I encourage you to take responsibility for your decisions and actions.

Keep in mind that how your child rates you is somewhat fluid. It may be influenced by a recent interaction and reflective of how she is feeling in response to that situation. While it may not always reflect how she would "score" you overall, it is a valid measure of how she is feeling at that time and a great springboard for discussion and action.

Deciding when to intervene in school issues and when to let your child decide how to address an issue more independently can be a difficult dilemma. While safety issues require no contemplation or hesitation—these concerns should be brought to the immediate attention of the appropriate school personnel—so many other issues can be inherently gray. There is no yardstick by which to measure how involved you should be. The spectrum of responses ranges from "Do not get involved! They need to learn to work through situations themselves" to "Get involved—contact the school always and often!" The key is to be informed about each situation and keep in mind the importance of taking a balanced approach overall. The following are some strategies to consider when fostering student-parent-child partnerships.

INSTEAD OF LISTENING TO JUST ONE SIDE, TRY UNDERSTANDING DIFFERENT VIEWPOINTS

Remember that, like all people, your child experiences every situation from his perspective. Absolutely listen intently to his explanation of a situation and then take some time to consider, together, who else was involved and what their perspectives are. Leading, however, requires realizing that other people and students might be experiencing the same situation differently. In a collaborative group project, for example, all the students may think they are doing all the work and no one else is doing their fair share. Work with your child to view the situation from her classmates' perspectives. Perhaps one student is doing *all* the brainstorming, while another is doing *all* the research, and yet another is doing *all* the writing. Students generally can work through disagreements on their own when given the tools to see beyond themselves.

INSTEAD OF RESPONDING TO IT, TRY *SITTING WITH IT*

Sometimes we have a knee-jerk reaction to situations. We want to jump right in and contact the teacher or solve the problem. But sometimes it is better to take it slowly. Stop and consider how urgent the situation is. This includes taking a moment to decide if your sense of urgency is being driven by emotions or because the situation itself is actually urgent. There is a difference. If your reaction is being driven by emotion, then abide by the 24-hour rule: Wait 24 hours before contacting the teacher. Sometimes a new day brings a new perspective. If the situation is urgent, then by all means, move full steam ahead. If the situation is not a crisis, take time to discuss the issue at hand and whether the teacher should be contacted. If so, determine whether email or phone is the better approach or if an in-person conversation is warranted.

INSTEAD OF FOCUSING ON AN INDIVIDUAL PIECE, TRY *SEEING THE WHOLE PUZZLE*

Sometimes we react to situations knowing only part of the story. You may have heard about an issue from one source, read only half of a memo, or misinterpreted an email. Don't rely on a single source that may not have all of the facts about a given situation. Seek out additional information and understand the big picture before jumping to conclusions and judging the teacher's or school's actions. Leading requires parents and students to be thoughtful consumers of information. If there is a school issue that you or your child feels strongly about, such as the availability of after-school tutoring or an art class being cut for budgetary reasons, seek out additional information. Why was there a change in the budget? What other school services were impacted? Who was involved in the original decision-making process? Armed with this information, you can become part of the solution.

INSTEAD OF BEING GENERAL, TRY *BEING SPECIFIC*

How often do you find yourself saying "Great job! I am so proud of you," or "You could try a little harder"? While these phrases are well intended, they are not particularly helpful. Good job at what? Was it the effort, attitude, end product, or the entire process? Children learn more when their parents are specific. Instead of telling the new driver in your family to "Be safe,"remind her not to text while driving and not to play the music too loudly. This same approach applies to working with your child's teacher. Simply letting a teacher know that you know your child can do better is not very useful. It is effective, however, for you and your child to share that she is struggling with persuasive writing and request assistance in that particular area.

INSTEAD OF RUNNING TO THE RESCUE, TRY *LETTING IT UNFOLD*

It can be tempting to drive the project your child left at home to school or to let your child off the hook for apologizing "just this one time"because he is so embarrassed, but in the long run, it is not doing him any favors. Certainly one must consider the larger picture, such as whether this is a habitual occurrence or unusual circumstances, and there are situations that warrant the drive to school. But you must be willing to take a step back and let things unfold. If your child continuously forgets his homework, rescuing him by delivering it to the school does not help him develop a sense of responsibility. Letting the natural consequences occur (staying in from recess to redo the assignment or getting points taken off for handing it in late) will help him understand the consequences of his actions and help foster responsibility. Whether it is a forgotten assignment or a forgotten cell phone, natural consequences are a meaningful learning process.

Commit to leading *with* your children. Parenting inherently requires patience, and this approach may even stretch it thin, but consider it good exercise. Not only does collaborative leadership lead to strong relationships and sound decision making in the present, but it sets your children up to make responsible decisions in school and throughout life's journey.

Leading Through the Years

This section presents ideas to help parents better understand and practice leading with children of various ages. As with all developmental recommendations, keep in mind that not all children fit neatly into their age category. Consider which descriptors best suit your child and follow the recommendations for that age range.

4- to 7-Year-Olds

Enjoy Parental Attention and Time

- Engage in fun projects with your children and demonstrate patience. This shared time sets the foundation for future partnerships.

- If you have more than one child, do some activities with each child alone.

Focus on Life at Home

- Involve your children in community projects such as neighborhood clean-ups or food drives.
- Begin a ritual of talking about school each day. Help your child problem solve daily school-based challenges.

Struggle With Issues of Fairness at School

- Listen to your child's concerns and help him see the perspectives of everyone involved. Be cautious to not take sides.
- Be open to meeting with your child and her teacher to discuss concerns in an age-appropriate way.

Enjoy Learning at School, but
Not Interested in Reading at Home

- Lead by example. Let your child see you reading books, magazines, and the newspaper. Continue to read to your child. When he is ready, let him read aloud to you.
- Make reading fun. Create treasure maps and scavenger hunts that require reading clues to find the hidden treasure. Act out plays.

8- to 10-Year-Olds

Progress to Structured Play With Peers

- As your child progresses from free play to more structured games with peers, help her understand the importance of shared expectations and establishing agreed-upon rules.

- Help your child understand and respect the viewpoints of others; this will help with problem solving when conflicts arise.

Begin To Be Aware of Community and World Issues

- Become active with your children in local volunteer opportunities.
- Encourage your child to use her voice at school on issues that matter to her.

Blame Others; Don't Take Responsibility for Actions

- Self-responsibility is a key component of leading. Help your child own the consequences of both positive and negative decisions.
- Share poor choices you made and what you did to address the consequences of those choices.

Want To Be Correct and Never Fail

- Ensure your child knows that it is okay to fail or be wrong. A great deal of learning comes from failure.
- Do not always let your child win a game or an argument. It is important for children to experience failing and how to respond to it.

11- to 13-Year-Olds

Feel Leading With Parents is Not Cool

- Be sensitive to the preteen years and the importance of peers. Be open to finding ways to spend time with your preteen that work for her.

- Stay involved with your children as a coach or school volunteer.

Realize That Their Parents Do Not Know Everything

- As students become more aware of their own knowledge and skills, create opportunities where they lead and you follow.
- Acknowledge that you do not know all the answers. Discover what issues are important to your child. Gather information and problem solve together.

See Socializing as a Priority

- Stay involved. Let your children know you monitor social media and decide together what is appropriate and not appropriate.
- Help preteens see the world beyond themselves. Even something as simple as watching the news broadens their views.

Fail to Recognize Long-term Consequences

- Discuss with your child her goals and ambitions and how the decisions she makes now impact her ability to reach those goals.
- Help your child understand how her actions can have positive and negative effects on her friendships.

14- to 18-Year-Olds

Seek Parental Advice on Broad Range of Issues and Challenges

- Parents may know something again! Try to discuss issues rather than simply give your solutions.

(Continued)

(Continued)

- Realize that your teen's insights and ideas may actually be better than yours.

Develop Greater Awareness of Inequalities and Injustices

- Encourage your teen to mentor younger students.
- Attend political rallies and other social awareness events together.

Act as Self-advocate

- Encourage your teen to speak up for herself at school and the work place.
- Be a sounding board when your teen is preparing to address an issue with an adult.

Feel Overloaded by Major Decisions

- Help your teen prioritize life's responsibilities and decisions.
- Work with your teen on creating a budget, putting together a resume, and filling out applications.

OUR LEARNING ABOUT LEADING

In addition to interviewing students, teachers, and principals, our work provides us opportunities to work with many parents in community forums and focus groups. We are fortunate to work in schools all over the country and overseas. During our journeys, we meet parents from all different backgrounds, races, ethnicities, family structures, etc. Perhaps one of our greatest joys is simply listening, learning, and hearing about how they lead. As we listen and learn from parents, we hear amazing stories of how parents, children, and schools work together to make school a more positive experience. In community after community, parents have helped us understand that the best way to lead with them is to know them in their communities. Three distinct examples stand out for us.

One high school in a rural community was frustrated by the lack of parental turnout for school events. No event, including sports, drew a crowd. School personnel tried holding raffles, offering supper, and even giving students extra credit if a parent showed up to an event. Nothing worked. The next attempt involved the students. As part of an English class assignment, the students were tasked with surveying and interviewing their parents to identify what was contributing to the lack of participation. Students analyzed the results in their math classes. The most common reason among the responses stood out clearly: The high school was located too far away from the neighborhoods where the families lived. No public transportation was available for families without a car, and the drive was up to one hour for families that did, presenting a challenge with both time and cost for gas. In addition, evening events could not be attended by parents who worked evening shifts. Informed by the results, school administrators reached out to parents via phone—no traveling to the school required! *Together,* they determined a solution: Quarterly meetings would be held in the four neighborhood elementary schools, alleviating the transportation challenge. Meetings for high school parents would also be held at the elementary schools in the morning, so parents who worked in the evening could attend. Only when parents, students, and the school collaborated was the issue identified, understood, and addressed effectively.

Another example of learning and leading with parents involves a school district with a predominantly Hispanic population.

One of the teachers, who was also a parent, invited us to her house for dinner. We were expecting a few people to attend. Boy, were we wrong! The whole neighborhood seemed to be there. Over the course of several hours, relatives dropped by nonstop . . . grandparents, aunts, uncles, cousins. Food was served the entire time and the conversations, in Spanish, never ceased. This was in stark contrast to the sound, or lack thereof, of parent participation in the schools. During meetings and conferences, very little was said by the parents; they mostly listened to the teachers and administrators. Two things occurred to us: 1. A relaxed environment where parents would feel more comfortable having conversations, in Spanish or English, must be created. 2. The parent-student-school partnership in this community should really be an *extended families*-student-school partnership. The entire evening reflected the importance of strong family bonds in this community. The room was filled with so much love and care. It was clear that if a teacher couldn't reach a parent on a given day, the teacher could call a student's aunt; and if the aunt wasn't home, he could call a cousin; and if the cousin wasn't home, he could call a grandparent. We learned from that dinner that any future efforts to lead collaboratively would involve a relaxed atmosphere and the entire family tree!

Finally, our work in one district brought us to the basement of a Baptist church, where I (RQ) had been invited to speak. I was immediately struck by how connected families were—to the church and each other. The sense of community and commitment was palpable. I knew from my work in the local schools that it was a struggle to get parents involved. I wondered how this could possibly be the same community. Everyone was clearly caring and invested here. This was the place they felt most comfortable using their voice—to communicate, connect, understand, and ask for and offer assistance. It made me think of the mentoring program we were trying to incorporate into the school district. We were having a difficult time getting volunteer mentors through our traditional avenues—emails, flyers, and phone calls. I brought up the mentoring program to the minister, and, without hesitation, he knew parents would participate. He was right. The program went from nonexistent to having a waitlist for mentors. Once the school connected with parents where they felt connected, shared leadership took hold.

We Are All in This Together

We have worked with tens of thousands of teachers over the course of our careers in situations similar to those above and many others. One thing we have learned for sure—these situations are no time to go it alone! Our experience allows us to confidently assert that it is extremely rare to find a teacher who does not want the same things as parents. They desire effective communication with students and parents, positive parental relationships, and the best possible teaching and learning environment that allows students to reach their fullest potential.

Yes, there are hurdles and perplexities to navigate, but a proactive approach to healthy relationships can lead to a successful journey. When parents, students, and schools are committed to working together toward a shared goal—helping students achieve their dreams—anything is possible. There are three prominent lessons we have learned from parents, students, and teachers when it comes to supporting voice. We should all be:

Listening more than speaking

Learning more than convincing

Leading more with others

CHAPTER 5

Staying in Tune With Your Child and School

While this book is wrapping up, the three of us feel we have only just begun. The more we wrote and revised this book, the more we learned about ourselves and our parenting skills (or lack thereof...). We reflected a lot, laughed a lot, and at times wondered how our kids turned out as well as they did with parents like us! The book also kept us real with our own kids. On more than one occasion, when I (RQ) made a decision that reflected less-than-stellar parenting, my daughter would say to me, "Is *that* in your parenting book?" As we mentioned from the start, this book was never intended to be a "how-to" book about parenting. It was written with the intent to provide an opportunity to reflect on your own parenting from a different perspective. It certainly did that for us. We would like to share our five biggest takeaways from this process. We hope they help you stay in tune with your children.

ACCEPT AND RESPECT THE FACT THAT YOUR CHILDREN HAVE DIFFERENT PERSPECTIVES THAN YOU

Parents and children have different life experiences and different personalities. They see, hear, and interpret things from their own perspectives. Add to the mix the fact that the society our children are growing up in is vastly different than when we were their age. All of this is okay—it is healthy and should be embraced. Clearly, our past is not our children's future. The one thing we do have in common is that we *feel* things in much the same way. Just like our children, we want to be loved, feel secure, and know we are valued for who we are.

PARENTS NEED AND DESERVE A MEANINGFUL ROLE IN SCHOOL

Parents unquestionably have a meaningful role in supporting their children's education. It is one thing to attend school events and parent conferences. It is quite another thing to be engaged in the teaching and learning of your children. We are not suggesting you become the new substitute teacher, but we are suggesting that your role in school has meaning and purpose that suits you and your child. Every parent, child, and school is different, and so an exhaustive list of possible "to do's" is impossible. Instead, we pose three questions for you to think about before becoming more engaged with your child's school:

Why do I want to get involved?

What do I want to get involved with?

What does my child think would be meaningful to become involved with?

Answer these questions for yourself before reaching out to your child's teacher and/or school administrator to see how you can contribute.

PARENTING SHOULD BE A PRIORITY, ALL THE TIME

Yes, sounds obvious—parenting is not a part-time job. Parenting is a full-time, all-the-time, lifetime profession . . . no retirement! But more than that, it is important to pay attention to *how* you spend your time with your children. Children get a bad rap for always being on their devices—texting friends, watching YouTube videos, or checking the score of the football game. In many situations, true enough. But the same can also be said for parents. Parents can get caught up in checking work emails or chatting with friends, and the time flies by. It is important for parents and children to not only be in the same room but to tune into each other rather than their devices. Staying connected with your children does not just happen. You need to *make* time to talk with and listen to your children and be fully present. Participate in the conversations—let your children know you are listening by asking questions. We understand you may be tired at the end of a long work day. So are your kids. School is their job, and they, too, have pressures that lead to fatigue. It is ok to just sit down and be tired together.

BE INTENTIONAL

Fortunately, some of what we do as parents comes naturally. Parents instinctively react when their child cries or laughs. Parents do not always have to think or plan ahead of time. Supporting and fostering voice, however, requires parents to be intentional—to find out *why* their child is sad, happy, or confused. Listening is an active process which requires focus and a genuine interest. Learning demands thoughtful questions and a belief that all children have something to teach us. Finally, leading together involves planning, practice, and purpose. None of which just happen. Voice is a powerful process that deserves effort and time to truly reap its benefits.

BE YOURSELF

The most important thing you can be as a parent is yourself. This does not mean you stop striving to be better at parenting, but you need to stay true to who you are as a person. It is not necessary to dress, talk, or act like a kid to appear more "cool." In fact, it is the opposite. You will be "cool" when you respect your children for who they are and remain true to yourself for who you are. Your children are going to love you for who you are, not for who you think you should be in order to win their approval. Your role is that of a parent, in the most loving, supportive way possible.

There is no doubt that parenting has changed over time. The previous punishment of "Go to your room!" has little effect unless elaborated on: "Go to your room and leave every single electronic device outside of your room!" The mentality of parenting has shifted from *"I don't care what it is, but you need to get a job and support yourself,"* to *"I want you to find a career that you're passionate about and do what is right for you."* Our role as parents has never been more challenging or more important.

Believe in yourself as a parent, and believe in your children. Listen, Learn, and Lead together. Above all, as a parent, never doubt that there are wonderful surprises just waiting to happen, and all your hopes and dreams for you and your children are well within your reach.

Index

Acceptance, 61–62
Adlee, 68–69
Advice, 38
Angelou, Maya, 49
Attitude, listening and, 30–31
Authenticity, 120

"Been there, done that", 71
Belief, 4–5
Big picture, 106–107

Change, 54, 80–81
Coaching, 102–103
Collaboration, 71, 85, 96, 108
Comfort zone, leaving, 72
Communication, 10–11, 58
Conferences, 98–99
Consequences, natural, 96–97, 107–108
Conversations, 11, 119
"Coolness", 120
Crab cakes, 66–67
Curiosity, 62–63

Decision making, 95–96.
    See also Leading
Down time, 40

Empathy, 28–29

Facetime, 11
Feedback, 107
Franklin, Benjamin, 51

Genuineness, 120
Goals, 91–93
Guidance, 38

Hemingway, Ernest, 21
Hobbies. *See* Shared experiences
Homework, 88–91
Honesty, 29–30, 120

Ideas, discussion of, 38–39
Independence. *See* Leading
Inquisitiveness, 62–63
Intentions, 1, 119–120
Interests, 25–26, 56–57, 59–61.
    See also Shared experiences
Interruptions, 47
Intervention by parents,
    100–101, 105
Introspection, 40
Introversion, 14–15
Invisibility, feeling of, 7

Judgment, withholding of,
    27–28, 40–41

Knee-jerk reactions, 106
"Know it alls", 71

Leading
    age of children and, 108–112
    balance in, 87
    coaching and, 102–103

considering all voices, 87–88
decision making and, 95–96
examples of, 112–115
importance of, 85–87
parent intervention and, 100–101
partnership development, 88–91
prioritization and, 93–94
proactive voice with, 97–99
responsibility and, 96–97
shared goals and, 91–93
skills for, 84–85
teamwork and, 94–95
tips for, 105–108
in Voice Model, 4
with versus for, 86
Learning
    acceptance and, 61–62
    age of children and, 74–78
    child rating of, 70–71, 79
    defined, 54
    importance of, 54–55, 65
    inquisitiveness and, 62–63
    interests and, 56–57
    letting child lead, 66–67, 71
    lifelong learning, 54, 80–81
    listening and, 51–53, 55
    mindful learning, 55–56
    new parents and, 68–69
    openness and, 63
    patience and, 63–65
    reflection and, 70, 73–74
    shared experiences and, 25–26,
      56–57, 59–61
    texting and, 57–59
    tips for, 71–74
    in Voice Model, 4
    willingness for, 16–17
Lifelong learning, 54, 80–81
Listening
    age of children and, 42–45
    attitude and, 30–31
    child rating of, 37

difficulties with, 23–24
empathy and, 28–29
honesty and, 29–30
importance of, 24–26, 49
learning and, 51–53, 55
meaning of, 22–23
mutuality of, 22, 26–27, 39–40
opportunities for, 32
practice with, 32
respect and, 27–28
strategies for, 37–42
tattoo examples of, 33–36
timing of, 41
tips from children about, 46–48
in Voice Model, 4
YIKES moments and, 21–22
Luccock, H. E., 83

Middle children, 88
Mindful learning, 55–56
Mindless listening, 53
Missing assignment dilemma,
    100–101
Mistakes, learning from, 72
Multitasking, 23–24

Natural consequences, 96–97,
    107–108
Noise, voice compared, 7–10, 19, 99

Openness, 63
Opinions, valuing of, 41

Parenting, 2–3, 119
Parent intervention, 100–101, 105
Parent involvement, 113–115
Parent-teacher conferences, 98–99
Participation, 25–26
Patience, 63–65, 106
Perfection versus progress, 73
Perspective taking, 105–106, 118
Power, 86

Praise, 107
Prioritization, 93–94
Progress versus perfection, 73
Promises, 23

Questions, 37–39, 119
Quiet time, 40

Reflection
    acceptance and, 62
    attitude and, 31
    child rating of, 104–105
    decision making and, 96
    empathy and, 29
    honesty and, 30
    inquisitiveness and, 62
    leading and, 104
    learning and, 70, 73–74
    listening and, 36
    openness and, 63
    patience and, 65
    prioritization and, 94
    respect and, 28
    responsibility and, 97
    shared experiences and, 60–61
    teamwork and, 95
    voice and, 17
Rescuing, 107–108
Respect, 27–28
Responding versus sitting with, 106
Responsibility, 12–13, 96–97, 107–108

Sarcasm, 28
Schools, 98–99, 118–119.
    See also Leading

Shared experiences, 25–26, 56–57, 59–61
Shyness, 14–15
Sitting with it versus responding, 106
Skype, 11
Sympathy, 28

Tattoos, listening and, 33–36
Teamwork, 71, 94–95
Texting, 10–11, 57–59
Three Ears to Success, 47
Trust building, 9–10, 30, 55–56
Twain, Mark, 66
24-hour rule, 106

Unfolding, 107–108

Voice
    consideration of all, 87–88
    noise compared, 7–10, 19, 99
    presentation and, 17
    as process, 9
    responsibility and, 12–13
    at school, 97–99
    self-assessment for, 18–19
    shyness and, 14–15
Voice Model, 3–4, 115. *See also*
    Leading; Learning; Listening
Volume, 15

Walking school buses, 95
White lies, 29

YIKES moments, 21–22

CORWIN
LEADERSHIP

Simon T. Bailey & Marceta F. Reilly
On providing a simple, sustainable framework that will help you move your school from mediocrity to brilliance.

Edie L. Holcomb
Use data to construct an equitable learning environment, develop instruction, and empower effective PL communities.

Debbie Silver & Dedra Stafford
Equip educators to develop resilient and mindful learners primed for academic growth and personal success.

Peter Gamwell & Jane Daly
A fresh perspective on how to nurture creativity, innovation, leadership, and engagement.

Steven Katz, Lisa Ain Dack, & John Malloy
Leverage the oppositional forces of top-down expectations and bottom-up experience to create an intelligent, responsive school.

Lyn Sharratt & Beate Planche
A resource-rich guide that provides a strategic path to achieving sustainable communities of deep learners.

Peter M. DeWitt
Meet stakeholders where they are, motivate them to improve, and model how to do it.

Leadership that Makes an Impact

A SAGE Publishing Company

Helping educators make the greatest impact

CORWIN HAS ONE MISSION: to enhance education through intentional professional learning.

We build long-term relationships with our authors, educators, clients, and associations who partner with us to develop and continuously improve the best evidence-based practices that establish and support lifelong learning.

Solutions you want. Experts you trust. Results you need.